WHY WE
FEAR

I0791658

ISBN 978-198-04-1821-4

© Henri Hyppönen and Kustannusosakeyhtiö Tammi, 2015

Translation Arttu Ahava

Cover design Jenny Sjödin

Kustannusosakeyhtiö Tammi, 2015

WHY WE FEAR

HENRI HYPPÖNEN

Prologue

1.

Jaws, by Steven Spielberg, premiered in 1975.[1] The plot is simple: an enormous great white shark preys on people on the shores of fictional Amity Island. The shark manages to chomp down a good number of citizens and holiday-makers before the city management admits that there is a problem.

The film is characterised by its ominous mood. The shark is rarely seen, but Spielberg lets the audience know that the great white is ready to attack each and every person who dares enter the water. The ominous art direction is accompanied by John Williams' chilling score.[2]

Jaws was a remarkable box office hit. It changed many things, such as Steven Spielberg's career prospects and the way Hollywood made films. However, Spielberg's bloodthirsty great white also had other, more long-term effects. Even though sharks have always spread fear among people, that fear was now carried to a new level. Even over three decades after the launch of the film, many

---

1 The script is based on *Jaws* by Peter Benchley.

2 The mechanical shark built for the movie affected the way Jaws was cut, as it was constantly out of action, and therefore Spielberg could not use it for all the scenes he had intended. As the schedule and the budget started to get tight, Spielberg made a decision: even when he could not show the shark, he would make the audience believe the shark was stalking unwary swimmers under the surface.

experts still believe that the film put a sizable dent in shark popula-
tions – due to the film, a great many sharks were killed.[3] Fishermen
headed en masse to sea in order to claim trophies of their triumphs
over these man-eating monsters. Shark-hunting competitions were
organised, with hunters participating without remorse – both the
competitors and the great public believed that they were doing a
public service. The shark was branded a vicious killer, and this brand
has not entirely faded even now.

Moreover, the film affected those who had no rational reason to be afraid: those swimming in lakes, ponds and swimming
pools. A cool current by one's feet or a suspicious shadow under
the surface of a lake would drive swimmers from the water. Some
did not even dare venture into a swimming pool if there was no
one else in the water. This kind of behaviour simply makes no
sense. The likelihood of dying by shark attack is so small that no
one should worry about it even when swimming in the sea.[4]
However, even if one were to intellectually accept that a lake, pond
or swimming pool is safe, it is no help whatsoever if one is afraid
that something is lurking under the surface or behind one's back.

All of this was caused by one movie, the star actor of which
was fear.[5]

---

3 For example, George Burges in an interview with *National Geographic* News said
that the US shark population sharply declined due to the movie, as thou

4 Likelihood of dying in a shark attack: 0.00003%. Source: "The Brain," *Discover
Magazine Special.*

5 In the words of shark expert Peter Klimley in an interview with Livescience:
"Everybody was scared senseless by that movie. It's very difficult to clear the memory and reset the mind." Apparently the fear of shark attacks is to a degree based on a
primitive fear of being eaten alive.

2.

Fear is far from being meaningless to people.[6] We experience fear because it is natural and because it has proven to be a very effective strategy for the survival of our species. It is a primitive feeling that carries out the most important of all tasks, i.e., keeping us alive and protecting us from danger. Fear is quite possibly the strongest[7] emotion, and the one that most affects human behaviour.[8] It defines almost all of our choices in life. Even if a person is completely safe, their threat assessment system is constantly active. It is ready to direct and to act immediately, once the signs of danger are detected. And these signs are indeed detected, as our brains and the related nervous system have been built in such a way that

6 However, there are at least two groups of people who do not know fear: sociopaths and those with damaged amygdalas.

7 There is still considerable dispute over whether people have universal emotions. For example, according to Paul Ekman people have only a few basic emotions, and the universal facial expressions relating thereto. These include, for example, fear, anger, joy and sorrow. In some cases, this list would also include surprise, shame, contempt and self confidence. However, for example psychology professor Lisa Barrett challenged Paul Ekman's findings by travelling to the Himba tribe in Namibia to show them pictures of people with a given expression on their faces. Unlike Ekman, she did not give her subjects any clues as to what was in the images, merely asking them to put pictures with the same emotion in the same pile. Barrett's findings deviated from those of Ekman. Participants mixed up hate, contempt and sorrow on a regular basis. However, she did get similar results as Ekman with two expressions: a smile and a fearful look.

8 A fear reaction can completely bypass one's conscious mind. It can sharpen or dull the senses in order to detect threatening objects, or even render one unconscious. Many scholars like fear precisely because it is a subject that can be easily studied and quantified. Fear-related bodily changes are strong, and it is easy to make a person learn fears. For example, fear memory researcher Daniela Schiller told me in an interview that one reason she picked fear as a subject was precisely the certain ease with which it can be studied.

detecting, avoiding, and protecting us from danger are prioritised over all other tasks.[9]

Each one of us makes a huge number of decisions every single day.[10] Some of our decisions are based on our genes, others on old habits, and yet others on learned models. Some are based on impulses and others on analytical reasoning.[11] In all of the above, our actions have at some point passed through a filter,[12] whereby the situation has been classified as safe, dangerous or life threatening.

Fear is connected to survival. It is no mere formality to bypass such an important thing. Fear, whether well-founded or completely imaginary, is always in play when it comes to human behaviour. Those who made decisions without fear, which is to say, without a fully operational defence system, were generally not able to propagate their genes.

---

9 The amygdala, the part of the limbic system that is particularly important for regulating fear (and anger) plays a key part in directing our behaviour. Information can reach the amygdala directly or through the cerebral cortex. Information arriving directly causes a fast, automatic change, while changes caused by information filtering in from the cerebral cortex can be affected. For example, you do not consciously decide to curl forward to protect your vital organs when you hear a loud, sudden sound. By the time you realise that the sound is harmless, your defence system will have already acted. However, this defence system is not purely reactive. It is on all the time and constantly assesses, based both on external information and information from within the body whether one is safe, in danger or in mortal danger, and commences the necessary preparations or more drastic changes required for preserving one's life.

10 The number of decisions is affected by what one considers a decision. The amount of conscious decisions, according to University of Columbia researcher Sheena Iengar, is approximately 70 per day, whereas no one knows the number of subconscious decisions. Estimates vary from several thousand to 35,000 per day. No wonder we feel so confused.

11 Which is likewise affected by feelings, no matter how much people believe they are rational beings.

12 Dr Stephen Porges calls this filter neuroception.

Let us consider this. If one Hollywood movie can make thousands of people panic in their swimming pools, how powerful must the influence of this force, so deeply ingrained in human nature, be on our daily behaviour, where we face many risks of varying severity. The problem of making decisions is connected with the finite processing power of our conscious minds. We can only process a fraction of the information that our senses provide.[13] Consequently, we have both innate (often automatic) and learned tools to help us make decisions.

People have two powerful tools to help manage risks: feelings and rules of thumb. Our feelings tell us whether to approach something or to back away. These feelings do not always cross the threshold of conscious thought, but often work on a sub-conscious level.[14] Rules of thumb, on the other hand, are conscious, often logic-based instructions learned either through our own life experiences or from others. They help us manage risks. Our feelings and rules of thumb often work hand in hand, preventing us from doing something stupid and helping to keep us physically and mentally safe. However, when allowed free rein, they can actually be a detriment. They can have a high cost for both individuals and society as a whole – never mind holiday swimmers and sharks.

Jaws serves as a good example of how fear works. It can mobilise the masses both in good and in bad, and make them do things

---

13 In my previous novel, Best Enjoyed Raw (2011), I explored the limited capacity of the conscious mind. Among many others, this subject has been studied for example by Karl Kupfmuller and Ap Dijksterhuis in their article "Think Different: The Merits of Unconscious Thought in Preference Development and Decision Making," *Journal of Personality and Social Psychology* 2004, Vol. 87, No. 5, 586–598.

14 Neurologist Antonio Damasio calls this a context feeling.

in the grip of emotion that, in hindsight, seem exaggerated or downright foolish. On the other hand, fear can also make people do things that are positive. In this book, I seek to illustrate the way in which these two are different: fear as a positive, motivating force and fear as a destructive influence that should be curbed.

Jaws also teaches us about how fear keeps people from doing things that would be of great benefit to them. When I asked my followers on Twitter how Jaws had affected their actions, one person gave an apt description. He had swum, without a cage, among tiger sharks in South Africa, and afterward asked himself: "What else have I missed out on because of fear?"

This book does not focus on sharks or swimmers scared by Spielberg, but instead on those everyday situations where fear is present – usually as an unwanted guest. Fear is there when we desperately need to be smart and creative, but our minds draw a blank; fear grips us when we stand in front of a live audience to give a speech; fear can dominate our lives at the workplace when the boss is a bully who needs to demonstrate his power over us.

3.

I told my friend that I was writing about fear. He felt that the subject was worthy but then immediately added that it was diffi-cult to write in concrete terms about fear. In people's minds, fear seems to present itself as some kind of ambiguous, magical power that appears to mess things up at the most inconvenient moment possible. Furthermore, fear seems to be something that we can do nothing about. In my view, this kind of thinking is not merely lazy but downright harmful. Fear is neither ambiguous nor amorphous, and it is far from magical. Fear is stealthy and contagious, but it is also a concrete phenomenon that can be grasped and controlled.

However, this can only happen once we start looking at fear as something other than a mythical or psychological phenomenon.[15] The real nature of fear becomes apparent when it is approached as a visceral phenomenon one that exists between people. Fear is manifest in the way in which our hearts pound, our palms sweat and people's voices seem to come from a long way off when fear takes control. The same thing happens for example when you are talking to someone and they suddenly start to act aggressively, scaring you. When seen in this light, fear can be disassembled into its component parts and its actions can be checked.

The first step in overcoming fear is to understand that fear is a word. Furthermore, it is a particularly complex word, which has different meanings for different people.[16] For that matter, scientists do not agree on what fear is. Psychologists, neurologists and biologists have several diverging views about the nature of fear. Not to mention various New Age gurus, philosophers, representatives of different religious groups, cultural anthropologists and security experts.[17]

---

15 And when one grows detached from one's feelings and examines one's experiences from an at least somewhat objective perspective.

16 In this regard, fear is like porn. It is hard to precisely define, but you know it when you see it.

17 Fear can for example be defined like this: as a state of activation of the amygdala, as an activation of the central nervous system, as an intuitive hunch or the triggering of atavistic defence mechanisms. For some people, it is an excessively vague psychological concept, while for others it is the root of all wisdom or the cause of all problems – the reason why one cannot travel to Venice, as there are too many pigeons there. Fear can be connected to thrill seeking, adrenaline kicks, abuse of power, obstacles to communication or a gut feeling that the man offering to carry your shopping bags should be turned down.

The word "fear" has been in use for a relatively short time.[18] Emotions, and after that feelings, evolved long before it.[19] They, in turn, came about only as a result of several billion years' of evolution, during which the central nervous system developed in a bid to secure the best possible chances for survival. All of these prehistoric mechanisms still exist in our bodies. They exist as nuclei and neurons in our brains, as nerve branches in our bodies and as hormones in our blood.

We human beings are different from other animals in that we have the capacity to worry about things that have not happened and indeed may never happen. We can even be afraid of things that do not exist, for example ghosts. We are a thoroughly fantastical species, as we are able to harness all of these ancient mechanisms in our own living rooms, where nothing threatens us. This is quite an achievement.

Furthermore, the power of words governs more than our own ability to think. Others can use this power over us. A politician, journalist or CEO who knows how to use words that trigger fear-related reactions can achieve a great deal. People consciously use fear without understanding its effects. I do not wish to claim that manipulation through fear has gotten out of hand. After all, humanity has always managed to find its own irrational and rational sources of fear during all ages of man. And yet, despite all our scientific, social and cultural progress, fear is still used as a tool to reach the most bizarre of goals.

---

18 At least compared to the age of the nervous system of defensive reactions, which we have inherited from lizards and mammals over a period of millions of years. Estimates of the age of modern man vary from 200,000 to 300,000 years. There is considerable dispute concerning the date when language evolved.

19 An emotion is a bodily state, while a feeling requires consciousness, which only developed later on. A feeling is conscious and can be put into words.

The original purpose of fear was to protect human beings from danger, i.e., to keep people alive in the extremely dangerous environments in which human beings and their predecessors evolved. Fear is excellent at this task, as very few gene mutations causing fearlessness have survived to this day through the harsh process of natural selection. There are a tiny number of fearless people and, as I will later show, their fearlessness carries a terrible price. However, fear is such a powerful and subtle influence that it is no longer confined to the role of protector but has instead grown into a monster. It turns up in unexpected places to mess with and influence things. Quite often, its work is hard to uncover – but not impossible. In this book, I aim to uncover the hidden mechanisms of fear and to find tools to tame and conquer fear where it has turned into a monster.

The practical effects of fear can be approached, for example, in the following way. Imagine that you are a tourist in Johannesburg, South Africa. You can find safety in that city of four million by knowing how to act. You should avoid moving around alone after dark. As a tourist, you should also steer clear of areas like Hillbrow, Alexandra, Soweto and Downtown. In order to stay safe, you have to restrict when and where you move. The assumption is that if you stay away from these areas and only move around during the day, you will be safe.

Put simply, fear draws this kind of map of our surroundings and the situations we are involved in. Fear is like a GPS, marking areas where you have to be careful and areas you should avoid. People generally have a fairly good idea about what they should avoid for example snakes, spiders, heights, aggressive people, arguments, maths tests and public speaking. However, not all sources of fear can be controlled through avoidance. Some of them refuse to stay fixed to a map. Let us imagine that you are still in Johannesburg, and you are for some reason afraid of birds. Pigeons, sparrows and gulls refuse to follow the borders of the city boroughs and instead go where they wish. However, as any real ornithophobe can tell you, there are places where there are more birds, and places with less birds.[20] In this way, Johannesburg (i.e., your living space) shrinks ever smaller. Even though birds do not necessarily directly threaten the life of a person afraid of birds, he or she would still rather avoid them. Moving around in Johannesburg turns into a threatening experience, as a pair of wings may be lurking around any corner, ready to disturb your peace of mind. The safe area on the map grows smaller, and as these sources of fear cannot be removed by avoiding them, the ornithophobic tourist is left in a constant state of alarm. Stress hormones and always active defence mechanisms lead to fatigue, and psychological stress hinders the cognitive processes. Now, take a step back and think of the pigeons as just one example of fear. They could instead be almost any other source of fear, for example fear of failure or fear of being revealed, fears that can be neither predicted nor avoided.

However, a tourist in Johannesburg is slightly different from our everyday contexts. Back home, this kind of mental map is etched deep into the dark recesses of our memory and embodied in our everyday habits. Fear no longer surfaces as powerful emotions and conscious thoughts but instead directs our actions on a far more subtle subconscious level. Alternatively, fear has been codified into rules, procedures and guidelines with good goals but a high price.

---

20 North Korea is probably an ornithophobe's paradise, as the malnourished people have killed so many of the local birds that, according to visitors, bird song is hardly to be heard in the country.

4.

In this book, I address fear in all its forms – both what people call fear and what scientists have determined to be fear.[21] In other words, fear includes both a state in which a person is worried, even though the source of fear is not present, as well as actual fear, where the source of fear is present.[22] If we look at Jaws, we are dealing with worry when the shark is not visible but we "feel" the threat of the shark, as well as with actual fear when we see the shark fin and hear John Williams' threatening theme song. Both states derive from the same part of the brain and affect the same parts of our nervous systems.

Just like Spielberg's great white, fear is a formidable monster that can either galvanise or petrify. A dash of fear can lend us energy, but too much fear for too long is poison; sometimes fear can help us while at times it hinders. Just like Jaws, this is a story about defeating a monster. This book, like Jaws, deals with discovering the nature of the beast, where it comes from, how it operates and – eventually – how it can be defeated.

I have also been attacked by this monster. It grasped my hands and feet when I was playing ice hockey as a teenager, as a sudden growth spurt messed with my coordination. It made me panic when I landed an internship at a local radio station ("What have I done, I'm going to have to talk to people"). It also struck me when, at my new job, a colleague fell sick and I answered "yes" when

---

21 Which is, for that matter, hardly cut and dry either.

22 Fear and anxiety are not the same thing. Joseph LeDoux, who has studied feelings in general and fears in particular, admits however that there is no clear distinction between the two, and both are connected to the same part of the brain – as both reactions are triggered by the amygdala.

asked whether I could cover for him in coaching a few hundred picky experts ("If only lightning would strike me!"). With age and experience, I have started to think of frightening situations as tests and tools of learning (yes, I still have to deal with fear), but when I was young I would have needed someone to tell me what I am about to say in this book: fear is normal, concrete and can be turned to your advantage.

In this book, I make a distinction between good and bad fear, and show how different people have suffered from, and made use of fear. I shall show how people have left behind the negative effects of fear through personal insights, and what scientists studying fear know about its different aspects.

Later on in the book, we will attack an adder, rise onto a speaker's podium, go through a bankruptcy, find out how many points of our IQ fear destroys, and how stupid we get as a work community when led through fear. On the other hand, we will learn how people have managed to confront their fear even at the brink of failure. I will show how fear is used to control people and to destroy their creativity, intellectual competence and ability to work together and furthermore how we can prevent that happening. I will also show how a sense of security can be returned, and how this new feeling of safety can be used to great benefit by individuals, teams and work communities, helping them think and act in a more critical and creative manner.

In this book, I want to turn fear into something visible and concrete, something tangible and malleable, to make people think about this remarkable force in a new way. How we would behave if we were not afraid?

Lunch Concerto

1.

"Like an electric shock." This is how conductor Riccardo Chailly afterward described concert pianist Maria João Pires' reaction upon hearing the first notes of Mozart's piano concerto No 20. Chailly had just swished his baton up and down, and the orchestra had started to play.

Mozart's piano concerto No 20, d flat KV 466, begins with the strings. Then the brass section plays for a while, followed by a brooding performance by the strings, alternating between frantic rhythms and pauses. Mozart and Chailly with his baton are setting the stage for the soloist. Both the public and the soloist are aware of this. They are also aware that, as this is a Mozart piano concerto, at Concertgebouw in Amsterdam and conducted by Chailly, there is no room for mistakes.

But why did Pires flinch? Let us imagine for a moment that you are in Pires' shoes, waiting on the orchestra stand for your turn. The concert hall is full, the orchestra is playing, and your solo, which the orchestra is leading up to, is set to begin in two minutes and 28 seconds. When it is time for you to start, everyone else falls silent. It is so quiet in the hall that even the smallest sound carries to the seats at the back. Often the mere thought of such an experience is enough to make our hands go numb and our mouth dry up. However, what could be the worst that could happen, if you discount standing there nude and dying in front of the crowd?

What would it feel like to sit up there, if you had rehearsed a completely different concerto than the one the orchestra were playing? This is precisely what happened to concert pianist Maria João Pires at Concertgebouw in Amsterdam in 1998.

Pires, sitting behind her grand piano, knew from the first notes that, in a little over two minutes, she would have to perform a small miracle. She had prepared for Mozart's piano concerto No 21, not piano concerto No 20 in d flat. She had made a mistake in writing down the name of the concerto.

The recording of the lunch concerto shows how the crowd of a hundred or so listeners waits for the orchestra to get to Pires' performance, leading up to it note by note. Pires smiles faintly, glances over her left shoulder at the violinist sitting there, and flashes her teeth in a half grimace. She presses her head down, raises it again, and tries to smile, but fails to maintain eye contact with the other musicians.

Pires presses her lips together and squeezes her eyes shut. Finally, she is frozen completely still. The problem is not that she would not know which concerto to play. She is quite familiar with it. Pires recorded the concerto in 1978 and has played it in public several times since then. The problem is that she needs to dig up the concerto from her memory and play it under extreme social and time pressure.

2.

Learning concertos by heart is part of the job for a soloist. This is not the difficult part. However, actually performing a piece from memory in a concert, under pressure, is so difficult that some pianists have found their career coming to an early end. Others never quite manage to reach their own level in a concert. A person's memory plays tricks when he or she is anxious.

There is something behind extreme anxiety and fear reactions, a system that, at its core, is intended to ensure our survival in threatening situations. All functions that are not at that precise moment crucial for survival are bumped down in priority or bypassed completely. The latest version of this system is, however, so old that it is mainly intended to protect us from direct physical threats. Deep thought has no value for our survival in a sudden, threatening situation, so it is ruthlessly neglected. This was extremely unfortunate for pianist Maria João Pires, as it prevented her brain from functioning at its normal level. The parts of her brain responsible for higher functions were probably inactive. Had Pires wanted to use these higher functions to find the right notes, she would have needed to stop the chain of events launched by her amygdala. This is because these processes were at that moment directing oxygen to where it was needed and preparing her body either for full-scale mobilisation or complete paralysis. Her head would have been either too empty or too full of thoughts.[23]

---

23 This is the reason why many of us can at a moment of extreme excitement feel like we are trying to explain a five syllable word using a children's playbook. The working memory does not function, as it is not essential for survival.

Luckily for Pires, she had practiced Mozart's piano concerto No 20 so many times that she did not need to remember her part, as it was stored in the lower sections of her brains, i.e., in what people call muscle memory. However, the chain reaction caused by the unexpected situation and social pressure had by then gone to her muscles. Her adrenaline glands were pumping adrenaline and cortisol into her blood, her heart was beating faster, and her blood pressure was rising. In such a situation, the body thinks that the large muscles need glucose and oxygen for fight or flight, rather than the fine motor skills needed to play Mozart. When the body prepares for fight or flight, it needs to raise its metabolic output, increase pain tolerance, numbing the sense of touch and decreasing surface blood flow. The muscles of the inner ear tense as the vagal nerve activates, making it harder to hear mid-range sounds. At the same time her central nervous system and certain cells inside Pires' brain releases noradrenaline, and even though it might help memory retrieval and focus, noradrenaline also brings restlessness and anxiety. These are pretty much exactly the kind of bodily changes that a pianist playing a piano concerto from memory does not want to experience.

Soon, it is Pires' turn. Her mouth is open and the small muscles of her cheeks are tensing. The orchestra plays the last notes. She raises a hand to her mouth, glances up from under her brows and then turns to the keys. The orchestra falls silent, and it is Pires' turn to play. She plays the first, delicate notes – correctly. Then the next few, again correctly. Then she launches into a part played at quick tempo, requiring great accuracy and manual dexterity. Again, she plays correctly.

Her part grows ever more complex, and the music seems to suck Pires into its flow. Now it is the orchestra's turn. Pires raises her face, looking anxious. When it is her turn to play once more, the miracle continues – Pires is suddenly one with the music once more. Soon enough, she has played the entire fifteen minute concerto flawlessly from start to finish.

3.

The fact that Pires managed this is astounding or at least rare. It raises questions about how she was able to navigate back from the fog and into the light. How was she able to switch off her defence system and play so gorgeously despite the pressure? And what can we learn about this in terms of controlling fear-based reactions?

Let us start with adrenaline and noradrenalin, which together formed one of Pires' greatest problems at that moment. Due to these chemicals, Pires' pulse quickened, in order to provide more oxygen and glucose-rich blood for her large muscles. Due to her increased cortisol levels, Pires' liver is able to provide large amounts of glucose for her body to turn in to muscle power. This would be great if her instrument was the gong, but Pires is a pianist known for her delicate and gentle approach to playing.

The 'half life' of adrenaline is approximately two minutes. Even though its direct effects would be short term after her adrenaline glands had stopped producing it, Pires had no time to lose. Her solo would start two minutes and 28 seconds after the first notes. It may be helpful to come up with a credible and constructive interpretation of one's own excitement. For example, a simple thing like interpreting a pounding heartbeat as anticipation can change the situation to your advantage, and overcome the fear monster.

Fear can make things more difficult in other ways as well. Fear-related anxiety can set off a chain of negative thinking. Concern and fear reduce cognitive capacity. A person may be rendered completely immobile in one of two ways: by entering an oxygen-saving state, which in plain English means freezing in place, or by thinking too much.[24] Even though the knowledge of how to play the concerto was deep in Pires' memory and she had practiced it so thoroughly that she did not need to think about moving her fingers, anxiety and fear reactions could still obstruct her from accessing this knowledge and expertise. This kind of state is not too different from the stage fright that we all experience from time to time: one's vocabulary shrinks, completely familiar things become hard to grasp and one's body moves in a stiff and unnatural way.

Even though Pires dislikes being categorised and denies being a Buddhist in this sense, she has never hidden her interest in eastern philosophy. Her grandfather, who raised her, was a Buddhist. According to Buddhist philosophy, you can set aside worries and concerns by focusing on the present. As a concert pianist, Pires had countless times been in situations where it is normal to be anxious. Now, in what was quite possibly the most demanding situation she had ever been in, she refused to run away, give up or search for her notes, and instead she shut her eyes.

Only Pires knows what she did or what was happening in her head. She may have been looking at things from far away, seeing

---

24 In *Overachievement*, John Elliot writes about this possible reason. According to him, too much is happening in the brain – in other words, overuse of neurons messes up one's performance, as too many brain cells are active at the same time. If this is the case, then it is quite different from an actual paralysis reaction, where the body goes into oxygen saving mode, and loses sensitivity as it prepares to undergo violence or a painless death.

herself from the perspective of an external observer. She may have been thinking that it was in the end not that big a deal if she were unable to remember the concerto. With nothing at stake, such as her reputation, money, income or her future, there would be no need to be tense. Pires may also have been focusing on her body, on her breathing, or on the music. In particular focusing on breathing in and out affects the readiness state of the body. A panic reaction can be stopped by slowing the rate at which you breathe out. These actions send signals to your nervous system, metabolism and various nuclei that nothing is wrong. What is in any case crucial is that Pires *did* something, and stopped the reaction from taking over.

4.

However, there is another protagonist in this story, which is to say conductor Riccardo Chailly, who was standing right next to Pires on the stand. Chailly detected the soloist's tenseness after the first time he moved his baton. The people filming Frank Scheffes' documentary *Voyage to Cythera* were not able to capture Pires' first reaction on tape, but they did record everything that happened after that. Pires manages to recover from her first reaction, and after 28 seconds have passed from the first notes, she looks at the conductor and tells him that she can try.

Chailly raises his gaze from Pires to the orchestra, and goes on conducting as if nothing had happened. Next, he turns his gaze to Pires, and says something that the tape does not catch. All of this takes place while he is conducting the orchestra. Pires explains something about her notes and how she left them in the wrong place. If one had to guess what emotion her body is conveying, it would be shame. It is an embarrassing situation.

In one minute and six seconds, the orchestra will stop and Pires must begin. Even though she seems to be struggling somewhere between anxiety and despair, Chailly encourages her: "You played it last season." Chailly looks at Pires, and smiles.

The concerto has reached a rhythmic stage where the orchestra plays forcefully. Chailly's body language seems to be saying that there is no problem, that the situation is in fact fun and exciting. "I'm sure you'll do it. You know that piece so well." Chailly punctuates his words in time with the music. He turns back to the orchestra, leaving Pires alone. She has 57 seconds to remember the piece. She closes her eyes and lowers her head. She raises her left hand in front of her mouth and nose, while the right moves, almost of its own accord, to the white keys. Pires opens her eyes and plays the first notes. She starts her part brilliantly, and plays flawlessly to the end of the concerto.

If this was a story about fear, then there were two heroes in it. One was Maria João Pires, who overcame her own defence system, and Riccardo Chailly, who instinctively or consciously helped to deactivate Pires' nervous defence mechanisms. Pires was safe, even though she was in a dangerous situation. Her amygdala was unable to transfer control over the body to the central nervous system, and adrenaline failed to mess with her fine motor skills. Pires' hands retained their sense of touch, she managed to fight off the rising panic, and the public got the lunch concerto they had come for. Bravo! This was a prime example of how one emotionally intelligent person and another socially intelligent person were able to together overcome fear. Ancora!

5.

One of the greatest fear-related misunderstandings is the notion that you can do nothing about fear. This is an understandable notion, but completely inaccurate. If you strip fear into its component parts, you can start to understand it. Fear has its history, its physiology and its psychology. When you have even a basic grasp of these various components, the different bodily reactions and the feelings and thoughts connected to them have less and less power over your day-to-day life. This is particularly important if you want to keep fear from destroying something important, whether that happens to be your peace of mind or a moment that is professionally of critical importance for you.

Of course, we could just label the story of Maria João Pires and Riccardo Chailly a miracle. However, even though there were elements of the miraculous about the concerto, nothing that happened inside Pires' head or between Pires and Riccardo is inexplicable – there is nothing here that any one of us could not learn. This same drama plays out in different settings in our lives, over and over again. We can all benefit from understanding the human and financial cost of losing to fear, and from knowing how to act in order to conquer fear – and reap the rewards.

Eagles and Doves and How They Are Made

1.

The Crystal Palace Eagles, playing in England's First Division, had the dream start for their 2003-2004 season. The team won their three first matches, leading the League. Then the team stumbled. Out of the next thirteen matches, the Eagles only won one. They lost eight, and four matches ended in a tie. In other words, out of 39 points, Crystal Palace only managed to get eight. The team's standing in the League at that time was by itself a catastrophe. The way they played those thirteen games was another.

The team was in a state of utter confusion. The players walked onto the field to win, but trying too hard, stupid mistakes and the resulting goals by the other side would quickly take the spirit out of them. Their eighth match to end in a loss was particularly humiliating. Wigan Athletic slammed five goals behind the Eagles' goalkeeper, while the Eagles scored nothing.

Eagles coach Steve Kember defended himself in the post-match interview, blaming the players for the bad result: "The talk has been about the pressure on me, but I am disappointed personally because in situations like this you expect the players to go out and do it for you." [25]

---

25 Ed Jones in *The Observer*, 2 November 2003.

Midfielder Aki Riihilahti was one of those who had had a bad match against Wigan. He had little to show for the game: a small injury and an early substitution. The players were disappointed as well, both in themselves and in their coach. According to Aki, the team expected and even hoped that their coach would be changed. They wanted a new beginning. Both team performance and mood were at their lowest point. "People were irritated, accusing each other, going it alone, not caring about common goals. A lot of people did not feel like they were part of the team," Riihilahti recently said, about a decade after these events. "I think many of us requested transfers to other clubs." Practicing did nothing to bring up the team's spirits. Mostly they dwelled on mistakes made in earlier games. The coaches seemed to believe that the team could win if they removed all mistakes from their game.

After losing to Wigan, Riihilahti joked with teammate Kit Symons that Kember would probably get the sack, and Kit would be made the coach, being the oldest and worst player on the team. Riihilahti's prediction turned out to be true. Kember was fired and Symons got a call.[26] It was from the owner of the club, appointing Symons the team's temporary coach. The Eagles were 20th in the league. It might be an overstatement to say that the team was in a panic. However, they were definitely worried, anxious and in a crisis.

---

26 Even though team observer Simon Jordan had promised Kember that he had a job for life with the Crystal Palace Eagles, the Wigan game was Kember's last.

2.

A game of football lasts 90 minutes.[27] During that time, one player has the ball for an average of 56 seconds. The rest, 89 minutes and 4 seconds, he spends preparing for his next contact with the ball. By taking the ball, a player can become a hero – or a public laughingstock. Just like that.

Football is serious business in the UK. Players are the objects of criticism off the pitch as well as on it, and there is nothing they can do about that. As it is a very public sport, the public criticism is unavoidable. Your successes and failures follow you to the shops, newsagents and pubs. The press scores players, and sports journalists turn the day's high scorers into stars, while presenting clinically precise – or at times wildly, maliciously inaccurate – analyses of the failures. Players getting good reviews may, for example, refer to an assessment by *The Sun*[28] when asking for more pay, as if stars given by journalists were scientific proof of how good their game was. What players may not always think of is that when the reviews (which are usually the general impressions of sports journalists) turn against them, the pressure starts to mount.[29]

For some players, the most difficult thing is winning the game

---

27 Plus of course injury time, which accrues due to various stoppages, most commonly injuries. Based on the players' reactions, it might look like most injuries require urgent orthopaedic care. However, players generally seem to undergo a miracle cure after having lain on the turf for a few moments.

28 *The Sun* is a major British tabloid, writing about celebrities, politics and sports.

29 According to some thinkers (from Nietzsche to sacred Buddhist scripture), a spiritually mature person ignores both compliments and scorn. They have the same root. If compliments touch your ego, then it means you are also vulnerable to insults. The door has been left open.

inside their own heads. One player who has publically spoken about this is Tony Cascarino, known for his long stretch playing for the Irish national team, who frankly discussed in his book Full Time how his inner voice ruined his career. Cascarino's inner voice was uncontrollable, frequently coming to haunt him in situations where he needed to focus on the game rather than on thoughts of failure. Cascarino's brutally honest book contains many examples of how his inner voice emphasised every weakness of his team and destroyed his confidence. After three bad passes, the voice would pile on the pressure: "One more pass like that, and that's it." Cascarino's inner dialogue was negative and out of control. He struggled to play a steady game. He could be in excellent shape early in the week, scoring a goal or two, and then play his worst game in the next match. Cascarino was prone to negative thinking, and as the tide of poisonous thoughts would grow strong, his game would collapse. Cascarino may have laughed at criticism by the press or his fans, pretending that he did not care, but in reality he was sensitive to criticism, and bad reviews stayed with him for a long time.

Then there are the fans, who are merciless – in particular the fans of the enemy team. The jeers of those sitting closest to the field are fully audible to the players – and they are mean. If a player has made mistakes on the pitch or outside it, he will hear about it. It is part of the nature of the game that you are not allowed to forget a class A blunder, and the social media certainly does not help. Thanks to fast internet connections and YouTube, your mistake can turn into a viral hit in minutes. You can make such a mistake in many different ways. You can miss an empty goal by miles, kick the ball right at the goalie on a penalty shot, or selfishly hang on to the ball when you should have passed. You can pass to the opponent, look like a fool because the opponent dribbled past you, fumble with an easy ball or make an own goal at the eleventh minute.

"Fear spreads. It's contagious," says Aki Riihilahti. You can see it in the players' body language and hear it in the coach's voice. Some might speak too much, while others fall silent. Many players show their anxiety already during warm-up. The body's fine motor skills and sense of timing weaken, so a player moves early or too late. He can no longer perform a pass that he has done flawlessly hundreds of times during practice. Fear takes its toll.

Most players have gotten into the sport because they like playing. But no one likes playing when the losses stack up. Talking to Aki about what happened to Crystal Palace in 2004 suddenly brought back a conversation I had with a professional ice hockey team that had been on a losing streak of 11 games in a row. At some point of the conversation, I asked them whether they remembered why they originally started to play hockey. There was a long silence. Finally, one of the players sitting slouched behind the table raised his eyes and said: "Because it's fun." Some of the others burst into laughter.

Losing time after time is hard. It wears down your self-esteem.

3.

It took a while for the owners of the Crystal Palace Eagles to find a new coach. Meanwhile, substitute coach Kit Symons created a foundation on which a new coach could build. In December 2003, former football professional Iain Dowie was chosen as the

Eagles' new coach. Symons turned over to him a team that had managed to score a few wins but that was still at the bottom of the league, ranked 19th.

At the time, Dowie looked more like a boxer or rugby player than a former top footballer. The big and burly Dowie first met the team at the end of December 2003, holding a speech for the Eagles. He announced that everything about the way the team practiced and played would change from that day on, and that someday the Eagles would play in the Premier League, England's highest football division. Dowie ended his speech by telling the players that "for the next two weeks, we are going to play football that looks like me. Ugly."

They immediately set about raising their level of physical and mental performance. The players were handed a weekly schedule of a kind that they had never had before. The coaching team indicated how committed they were to the players by their attention to details. When the team arrived for practice, the coaches would already be there, and the equipment needed for the first exercise would be set out on the field. These small but important acts built trust between the coaches and the players.

Dowie brought with him John Harbin, an experienced fitness coach and sports psychologist. The team practiced harder, smarter and more diversely than before. Besides football practice, the players also beat punching bags, danced and swam. They started holding voluntary "self development Wednesdays." The daily schedule usually included a film or a story. The coaches would go over the stories of people or teams who had struggled from being the underdogs to victory. The coaches were laying out a new story for the team. This time it was not about avoiding mistakes but about rising from the bottom.

Dowie's first match was not particularly promising. It was a local game against Millwall at the Eagles' home pitch at Selhurst Park. Almost 20,000 spectators came to watch the new coach's first game. However, to the disappointment of the fans, the match ended in a 0-1 loss for the Eagles. However, the way they played had completely changed. The team no longer looked like the group who had lost so shamefully to Wigan almost two months ago. The Eagles were now playing good football. Things looked promising.

In addition to developing their physique and football skills, the team's mental state was also improving. After this first loss "our game opened up," in Aki Riihilahti's words. First they beat Ipswich Town, then fought Burnley to a tie, and then crushed their opponent 1-5 in an away game at Watford. The Eagles won seven matches in a row. The team climbed up in the league table toward a playoff spot. The Eagles won no less than 14 of the 22 games they played under Dowie. Out of 66 possible points, the Eagles took 44. By the time the whistle blew on the last match of the series, a miracle had happened. The team had risen to number 6 in the league table. The Crystal Palace Eagles were in the playoffs.

In the playoffs, the Eagles were up against Sunderland, number three in the league.[30] The Eagles won the game 3-2 without going into overtime. The next match at the Sunderland home pitch ended in a tie, 1-1, followed by a nerve-wracking shootout, which the Eagles won. A second miracle had occurred. The Eagles had fought their way to the First Division final.

---

30 The first two, Norwich City and Wes Bromwich Albion, rose directly to the Premier League.

The Division final was played at the massive Cardiff arena in front of 75,000 spectators. The match was even, with the only goal scored by Neil Shipperley. When referee Graham Poll blew three times on his whistle to signal the end of the game, a third miracle had happened. The Eagles had won the final and a place in the Premier League. Heaps of people, celebrations, raised fists, U2's Elevation, pyrotechnics, fire-works, confetti and the championship cup in the upraised arms of scorer Neil Shipperley: "C'mon, beautiful isn't it?" [31]

4.

The press were as surprised as everyone else, and ended up coining a new word for the team: "bouncebackability." Dowie and John Harbin had done something incredible. A team mired in a deeply defensive way of acting and thinking had been turned around, and brought right to the top. How?

According to Aki Riihilahti, one of the key factors was that the new management built new, professional routines for the team. Physical and mental exercise was greatly increased. Everything was done systematically. During practice, players concentrated on honing their own skills and expertise, and no time was spent poring over the mistakes of past games.

In addition to carrying out radical changes, the new coach spent a great deal of time with the players, talking about their wishes

---

31 While Neil Shipperley and Simon Jordan could not have been happier, their opponent West Ham was full of disappointment. Hayden Mullins was particularly disappointed, as he had requested and gotten a transfer from the Eagles while the team was at the bottom of the league.

and goals and about their lives outside the pitch, such as their families. One key factor in building mental fitness was feedback. Dowie gave detailed feedback and encouraged the players. He built up their self-esteem by focusing on the things that they were good at and helped them to notice the simple things in which they could improve. The players did not have to play a guessing game of what the coach had seen on the pitch and whether he valued his players. From his feedback, the players could tell how much the coach cared, and how much time and energy he had spent on them.

Before every match, the players would receive a sheet of A4 paper from the coach. On the top row would be the names of the two teams playing against each other. Below that would be the name and position of the player, as well as playing time.[32] The next three rows would be numbered, and there the player would write his own aims for the next game. At the bottom of the page would be a different quote for each game. Most were familiar to the players from "self development Wednesdays," such as the Adrianne Rich quote: "Courage is not defined by those who fought and did not fall. It is defined by those who fought, fell, and rose again."

After each game, the players would dig out their sheets of paper and grab their pencils again. Each sheet had two more boxes, labelled "personal evaluation" and "team evaluation." The players would write their own analyses of the events of the game. In the evaluation fields they would write a score from 0 to 10 for both themselves and their team as a whole. Finally, the papers would be returned to the coach, who would write personal feedback for every player for that game.

---

32 The last of these was naturally filled out only after the game.

The one thing that is striking about Dowie's feedback is how precise – but on the other hand safe — it is. When he compliments a player, he states precisely what he did well. When he gives constructive criticism, he also explains what needs to be improved. Dowie's feedback centres on two important areas: the player's performance on the pitch and his attitude. "You looked hungry and strong," "Brilliant morale and much better focus on defence" and "Once again you did the dirty work of the team on the pitch very well, but you looked a little anxious and did not ask for the ball. You intercepted a lot of key passes. That did not go unnoticed."

Dowie also often had a Yoda-like attitude to the actual end result of a given match.[33] The team and the players could not fail. Things were what they were, no matter who did what, and the result was the result, however a game ended. Overanalysing or overreacting was pointless.

To an outsider, it looks like Dowie used every means available to try and lower the stakes. This is one of the key ways of trying to make a fear-struck team, company, group or individual work at the extreme limits of their abilities.

Think of it like this. Few people have a problem walking along a half metre wide line through a parking lot. However, if you raise the line twenty metres in the air, the stakes become so high that many will grow unsteady. Mental stakes have the same effect. For example, if a player feels that a game must be won or that he must show his new club how good he is, avoid shame, try not to make mistakes, or keep from showing his

---

33 Yoda-like is similar to Zen-like. Those who are not overly sensitive to Zen can substitute for example Dalai Lama-like or Suzukiroshi-like for Yoda-like.

anxiety to the fans, all of this can trigger a fear-based defence mechanism.[34]

Usually a group of players, a team at the workplace or an individual whose defence mechanisms have already taken over will not benefit from additional pressure. The Eagles' coaching team very wisely saw this, and decided to cut off the poisonous thinking.[35]

Dismantling these defence mechanisms also had other effects. Once the crisis had passed, people had enough energy for doing things together. Someone brought new gym gear, the dining hall was done up with the team colours[36] and the team decided to fix the club house showers together. Before, only two out of ten showerheads had worked. While they did not turn their showers into a luxury spa, at least the showers worked. Team morale was booming on all levels.

"I remember how Tommy Black brought a bloody big bouncy castle and kids' party hats, so we could celebrate the birthdays of two players for five minutes before practice," Riihilahti says,

---

34 However, some people seem to be immune to pressure, or actually get a kick out of it.

35 Some players had their own ways of breaking free from their own and others' excessive expectations. Aki Riihilahti is one example. When he was very young, he understood that he was not an exceptionally talented player. However, he was a hard worker and could be top class in a certain narrow area, while delivering a good performance at what he was paid for. Aki also has a strategy for when things do not go as planned. Through practice and conditioning, he has created a safety net to which he can return, a playing foundation that never wavers, and on which he can build and improvise.

36 We watched some videos from that season with Aki Riihilahti. On spotting the team canteen, Aki burst out laughing. It was only now that he realised that table cloths had been brought to the canteen in red and blue, the team colours. What was important was that the canteen was decorated by team members. Wonderful things were happening in the team.

recalling the change that took place in the mood of the team. The players took up the slogan "Sometimes beaten, never conquered"[37] for the team, and had a print made of it, hanging it on the wall of the club house. Some players would cut individual quotes from the speeches of Muhammad Ali and fix them to various places around the stadium.[38]

Perhaps at this point it would be a good idea to recall pianist Maria João Pires and conductor Riccardo Chailly. Chailly calmed Pires with his manner, and managed to get her to stop her defensive reaction. Even in a hall full of listeners, Pires felt safe with Chailly. As we will see later, there is a reason why we behave differently when we are safe than when we feel threatened. These reasons are also not purely mental or emotional, but derive from the nervous system. When our defence system is not involved, messing things up, the required higher functions such as fine motor skills, sense of rhythm, the ability to make observations, creativity and other cognitive functions are wholly at our disposal. Blood flows to those areas that are most important for that performance, the mind focuses on the task at hand, the fear systems become less active and our emotions fade into the background. Iain Dowey and his co-coaches worked hard, carefully creating an environment without fear. They chained the monster and set their team free.

---

37 *Sometimes beaten, never conquered* is the name of Australian star runner Raelene Boyle's biography.

38 The mood and the slogans also caught on with the fans. The words chanted by the crowd of the Ali vs George Foreman match, "Ali, Bumbayee!" ("Ali, kill him!") were shouted at Selhurst in modified form: "Aki, Bumbayee!"

5.

Usually a company operating at a loss does not act like Iain Dowie's Crystal Palace Eagles when it tries to rise back up. Kember's term is more indicative of what often happens in companies and teams that are in a downward spiral. Once the company is doing badly, people easily focus on mistakes – which is what Kember did. During practice, they focused on correcting mistakes, which is to say going over the failures of the previous games and wondering how to correct them. Dowie's model was different. During practice, the team would prepare for the next game, and players would know how to change their performance based on very detailed feedback. This was crucial. If a person's self-esteem is already in ruins, then focusing on mistakes only confirms the player's low opinion of himself and his abilities. Self-esteem can be bolstered through success. Dowie arranged things so that players got to experience small successes during practice. You can create exactly the same environment in companies. This requires forgetting the bottom line for a moment and emphasising small, concrete actions that everyone can do. Dowie was not interested in the end results of the matches, which also took some of the pressure off the players. The stakes were no longer being raised. People were focusing only on what they were doing, rather than factors partly or completely out of their control.

The public to-and-fro accusations, which had torn the team apart, also ended with the change of coaches. The mutual trust inside a team will immediately suffer if it becomes apparent that management does not want to take responsibility. Mutual trust can also be endangered for other reasons, for example if people communicate in a hostile way due to frustration. This will lead to a collapse in the amount of communication between group members. In the business world, a decrease in communication and the creation of cliques can be even more dangerous than in team sports. In team sports, poor morale or a negative atmosphere evidently leads to poor results. Meanwhile in companies, the importance of an open atmosphere and sense of trust and worthiness may often go unnoticed – but it is crucial for doing things smartly. Creative problem solving, performance speed and getting the information necessary to overcome a challenge all become difficult when people are no longer meeting each other or are afraid to give information to each other that might weaken their own position in the work community.

When problems in the work community eventually arise, a poor atmosphere or weak sense of community means that the best people generally start looking for a new job in another company. This is what happened in Crystal Palace before Dowie set in, and this is what all too often happens in companies.

Once the external pressure mounts up and the company is in crises, management often shifts the pressure onto the staff. Spreading awareness of the crisis does not help, however, if people are already anxious or afraid. Even though it is important to give an accurate picture of the situation, it is one of management's most important tasks to make individual employees feel safe enough that they will continue to carry out their work creatively and at a high intensity. Iain Dowie accomplished this by spending a lot of time with his players. A manager often cannot promise what the future will bring, particularly in the age of unpredictability that started with the Subprime crisis.[39] However, a manager can be there for the employees, showing them how much he or she values and supports them, and spending time with them as a person, rather than just as a manager.

What is most important is that Dowie offered the team a new story. During Kember's term, the team concentrated on fixing mistakes. In terms of classical stories, Kember would have been, through his actions, telling the story of a beast and how to conquer it. This is also what many CEOs do. The beast can be a recession, structural change, digitalisation or the transfer of labour to cheap countries. Conquering the beast can be a rousing story, if the situation is short term. However, let us stop and think about what this story is about. Jaws is a typical example of a story about defeating a monster.[40] Once the shark has been killed, the mission is accomplished and the end credits roll down. However, we never get to see the heroes return home to the town. Furthermore, that town will never be the same. Friends, children and tourists have been killed. When someone looks at the beach, their first thought will not be a seaside vacation but the tragedy that occurred there. The environment is full of triggers for fear-related memories. A story about defeating a monster is not always optimistic, and we recognise this on an instinctive level.

---

39 The financial crisis that started with the US sub-prime mortgage crisis of 2007-2009.

40 The theory of story types is from Christopher Booker, according to whom there are only seven basic plots: overcoming the monster, rags to riches, the quest, voyage and return, comedy, tragedy and rebirth. Booker's theory is explored at length in his mammoth volume *Seven Basic Plots* (2004).

However, Dowie told his team a very different kind of story. In practice, he told and retold the players the story of Cinderella, i.e., the classic rags-to-riches story. Through his anecdotes, Dowie showed the team how you could overcome difficult circumstances. Even though your company or team might not struggle through a difficult period only to end with victory celebrations and champagne, a rags to riches story seems to communicate that even small improvements are victories and setbacks are only temporary. It is an important story about learning.

6.

Conductor Riccardo Chailly and football coach Iain Dowie have a functional model that leads to great results: restoring people's sense of security, reducing excess pressure, restoring self-esteem, building a constructive interpretation of the facts, inspiring people and focusing on simple, concrete things. In addition, this is a very human model, but it is not about being soft or encouraging positive thinking while ignoring the facts. Even though Chailly and Dowie faced different circumstances, both started from the facts.

Pires was in the middle of a live performance before an audience, and she had rehearsed the wrong concerto, which was not something she could change or affect. Instead, Chailly and Pires concentrated fully on what was actionable and turned the focus away from the negative emotions, especially fear, that were preventing Pires from accessing the information and skills needed to perform the unrehearsed concerto. Chailly encouraged Maria João Pires, telling her that the right notes were there in her memory, and it would in the end not be such a big deal if she failed. It was the best thing Chailly could have done to help Pires during the extremely limited time available. Dowie also spent time reducing the stakes and restoring his players' sense of safety. In addition, he came up with a demanding physical programme and routines for his team, which by themselves created continuity and a sense of safety.

A management style that emphasises this kind of safety and improvement by small steps is something that we ought to see much more often in today's working life, where dwelling in a negative spiral of losses and in an atmosphere of fear have become the norm. It is quite understandable that even the management get frustrated in a difficult situation. It is also understandable that aggressively addressing mistakes seems intuitively like the right way to respond. If there is a problem, it can be rectified. However, even if this may intuitively seem correct, it does not appear to produce much in the way of results. It is in any case not the only way out of a negative spiral.

Let us return to working life, but first we will dig deep into the mechanisms, into the biology of fear. We will look at how these mechanisms can be used and how to avoid letting the cost of fear become too great to bear. First we will come face to face with an animal that almost always manages to activate the fear coded into our genes.

Darwin and the Adder that licks your ear

1.

The adder is the most common venomous snake in Europe. It is particularly known for the distinctive zigzag pattern on its back. Adders are deaf but have a keen sense of smell, allowing them to find their prey: mice, moles, frogs and slowworms. The adder hunts and defends itself with its needle-like poisonous fangs and the hemotoxin secreted from those fangs. It is perhaps this venom that makes the adder such a bad animal in people's eyes, in addition to it being a snake.[41] Adder venom has two survival-related tasks: it kills prey and commences digestion before the meal has been swallowed whole, and it scares non-prey animals that might otherwise threaten the adder. Biting is also a defensive reaction whereby the adder's ancestors survived to pass on their genes. Adder venom can in theory be fatal to a human being, but adder-related deaths are extremely rare. The venom is not significantly more potent than that of a wasp, and the adder carefully regulates how much venom it uses when defending itself. While it is true that you should be careful around adders,[42]

---

41 The hemotoxin in a snake's venom glands destroys tissue, red cells and the walls of blood vessels. It also causes blockages and necrosis of blood vessels.

42 One should wear boots in areas with adders. If you intend to pick up an adder, wear long sleeved, thick leather gloves, such as those worn by welders, and which cannot be pierced by an adder's venomous fangs.

it is nevertheless a relatively harmless species for human beings. The adder is not aggressive, nor is it particularly fast. Nature is full of creatures that are much more dangerous for humans, such as moose, ticks and wasp, which kill people every year, unlike adders. However, thinking of a moose or a wasp does not send shivers of revulsion down our spines. Our reaction to the adder is also not tempered by the fact that the people die every day doing everyday chores, in traffic accidents, by choking or through electrical shocks.

Snakes and fear reactions have a long history of scientific study. The horned viper, a distant relative of the adder, was the unwitting tool whereby Charles Darwin formulated his ideas of human defence mechanisms. Darwin attempted to overcome his own nature in the face of horned viper attacks – and failed. Writing in 1872, he looks back to the time when he stood in the London Zoo in front of the horned viper terrarium. Even though there was thick plate glass between him and the snake, he was unable to keep his head still when the viper struck at the glass. Willpower and a solemn decision to stand still were of no use. When the horned viper attacked, Darwin leapt back.[43] Fear made his muscles move independent of his will. From his experiences, Darwin drew the conclusion that our fear reactions are not guided by our conscious minds, but that there are ancient structures deep in the human brain that trigger these mechanisms. In this, Darwin was ahead of his time, as the mechanism he had discovered was only scientifically proven in 1939, when brain surgeons Heinrich Kluver and Paul Brucy conducted experiments on apes.

---

43 Darwin wrote about this in his *The Expression of the Emotions in Man and Animals* (1872).

They discovered that if you removed certain parts of the brain, it would radically change the fear behaviour of the apes. However, it was not until 1956 that Lawrence Weiskrantz observed that merely removing the amygdala would cause the same changes in ape behaviour.[44] The animals became fearless.

Scientists still disagree on whether fear of snakes is learned behaviour or hard-coded into our genes, with views both pro and con for both options. However, the hard fact is that the snake is one of the most feared animals[45] and that people get shivers of fear just looking at pictures of snakes, even in areas where there have never been any snakes.[46] If two people need to find something in common, fear of snakes seems to be a strong candidate. Therefore, it feels bizarre to meet someone who, every summer, lets adders get close enough to his face that they can lick his nostrils.

2.

April 1962. Urpo Koponen, a schoolboy in Jäppilänkylä in eastern Finland, got lost during an orienteering competition. He sat down

---

44 Weiskrantz, L., "Behavioral changes associated with ablation of the amygdaloid complex in monkeys." *Journal of Comparative and Physiological Psychology*, Vol 49 (4), Aug 1956, 381–391.

45 For example, in an international study carried out by Graham Davey's group, the snake was in category of the eight most-feared animals: the lion, the bear, the alligator, the crocodile, the tiger, the wolf, the shark, the squid and the snake. Davey, G.C.L. et al., "A cross-cultural study of animal fears," *Behaviour Research and Therapy* 36, 1998, 735–750. Many internet sources refer to fear of snakes as one of the most common phobias, but rarely cite sources for such a statement.

46 Even if evidence might seem to give a clear answer to the nature-versus-nurture debate, the most likely explanation is that, rather than snakes (and spiders) per se, our genetic heritage has been imprinted with a fear of anything that seems danger-ous. The evidence is gradually accruing for this theory.

on a giant boulder on the nearby rocky hill of Töytärkallio to rest his feet. His rest was interrupted when the earth started to move a few metres below the boulder. There was an adder highway right under his feet. It was not a pleasant sight, especially as Koponen was afraid of snakes. An adder had bitten his friend, and after that Koponen had developed a fear of the reptiles. However, as he was sitting high on the boulder, there was no immediate danger, so little by little curiosity overcame disgust. Koponen started to count the snakes, marking them in his notebook. There were almost two hundred adders. Even though this changed his attitude toward adders, the biggest change was yet to come.

As a place, Töytärkallio seems almost to have been made for cold-blooded reptiles. It is a rocky scree slope with no trees and plenty of light.[47] The sun warms the snakes that slither onto the boulders, and there are plenty of hiding and nesting places among the rocks. It is also an ideal spot for a snake photographer like Koponen. He has particularly strong memories of one session and one photo of an adder in summer 1997. He wanted to take a photo of the moment when the first adder of the day peeks its head from its nest. However, he had to be there before eight in the morning to get the shot. Adders keep a very regular schedule, and tend to do the same things at the same time from day to day. Koponen arrived early at Töytärkallio, and lowered himself next to a boulder, at the entrance to two adder nests. However, it was

---

47 I met Koponen in Kotka, where we went to Töytärkallio. There are hundreds of adder nests there, and even though I was writing a book about fears and conquering fears, I was happy as I walked between the rocks where we had arranged the interview for (8 January 2014) while the snakes were deep in slumber. According to Koponen, snakes love places like Töytärkallio. Power lines run over the rocks, with trees cleared around them. Consequently, the cold-blooded reptiles can get plenty of energy from the sun, i.e., warmth.

not yet eight, so he dozed off on the moss. "About an hour later, Koponen woke to an odd sensation: one of the adders that had crawled out of the nest was licking his ear.". Koponen was tense and anxious, frozen in place trying to second guess what the snake would do next. Would it see him as a threat and bite? Would it slither into his clothes? "I mustn't move now," Koponen thought. Sweat dripped from his forehead. Meanwhile, the adder was quite calm. It licked Koponen's neck and then slithered away.

It turned out that Koponen had been filming snakes the wrong way for the last twenty five years. Koponen, a big man, had tried to sneak up stealthily to where the adders would be waiting. However, sneaking is pointless, as adders do not, against common belief, care about vibrations in the ground. However, snakes are alarmed by tall shapes nearby. Even when Koponen managed to sneak right up to the snakes, they would quickly dart to their hiding places once he started to take photos from high above.

For a successful photo, perspective is key. Adder photos taken from ground level are exceptional. The only problem is that you have to be face to face with the snake to take them. Koponen would put on a motorcycle helmet and lower himself to the same height as the adders. The closer he got to the ground, the less wary the adders were of him. Curious adders would poke at his helmet, but after a while they would leave it alone. Soon, the helmet felt not so much like a shield but more like an obstacle that got in the way of the photos. Koponen gave it up.

The first time was the most difficult. The adder came so close that it licked the nostrils of the photographer, who was frozen stiff in front of it. Koponen remembers wondering how on earth he was going to get out of that situation. However, once again, after a while the adder retracted its tongue and slithered away.

For Koponen, getting used to being touched by snakes was the hardest part. It took him three years. He has called this a process of building tolerance. He believed that his defensive reaction would eventually weaken, and this was indeed what happened. Now Koponen's natural defence mechanisms are not triggered even when an adder slithers between the camera and his face and occasionally licks his nose.

Building tolerance is unpleasant, but it works. The idea is very simple: you face the source of your fear so many times that the mechanisms responsible for keeping you alive no longer trigger alarms. This is not just snakes, though it is particularly effective with them, as even a phobia can be treated effectively by gradually exposing the patient to the source of his or her fear. Building tolerance works with any overactive fear reaction. Koponen found out on his own that, if he could make himself lie there in front of an adder without facial protection, his defence system would eventually get used to it. Now, thanks to two Israeli researchers, we also know what was happening in his brains.

3.

Uri Nili and Yadin Dudai are researchers at the Israeli Weizmann institute. Through their work, we can see what was happening in Urpo Koponen's brain at the moment when he decided to sprawl down to face the snakes. Nili and Dudai managed to get 39 people with an exceptionally strong fear of snakes into their laboratory.[48] The participants would lie down in an fMRI

---

48 We should bear in mind that people in the Middle East have real reasons to be

device[49] in order for the researchers to see what was happening in their brains while they carried out their unpleasant task. The snake averse participants were told to lie down next to a conveyor belt, with a 1.5-metre corn snake at the other end.[50] Their instructions were to use a game pad to pull the snake as close to their heads as possible.

For all test participants, their amygdalas lit up like candles in a dark room the moment they started their assignments. As they were asked to move on to the next phase, i.e., to move the corn snake closer or further away from themselves, other areas were activated. However, this only happened for some participants,[51] i.e., those who pulled the snake closer to their heads. These brave participants helped the researchers get a glimpse of what happens in the brains of a person who is overcoming his or her fear. A particularly interesting area was the one that brain research-

---

afraid of snakes, which kill dozens of people every year. Of course, this is small fry compared to India, with 10,000 – 15,000 deaths per year. These figures are from the IST (International Society on Toxinology) international snake bite statistics, based on research by Wickremasinghe, A.R., de Silva, N., Gunawardena, N.K., Pathmeswaran, A., Premaratna R, Savioli, L., Lalloo, D.G., de Silva, H.J. "The global burden of snakebite," 2008.

49 fMRI, i.e., functional magnetic resonance imaging is a medical imaging method whereby the brains are charted by examining how blood oxygen content changes in different parts of the brain for example while the subject is carrying out various assignments.

50 Test participants lay down in the device in turn, while researchers stuck sensors to their skin in order to measure electricity conductivity. Then they asked participants to grasp a joystick, used to control a conveyor belt running next to their head. The corn snake is not venomous, but all test participants were sensitive to snakes. One participant grew so hysterical that the test had to be stopped.

51 Those subjects who were quite simply unable to pull the snake closer to their face did not have activation of the sgACC area. Their amygdalae lit up and they were sweating like crazy, but their sgACC area stayed cold. The conveyor belt came very close to the subjects, who could if desired pull the snake within twenty centimetres of their face. Few of us would want to be that close with even another human being.

ers call the sgACC, which is to say the subgenual anterior cingulated cortex. The sgACC seemed to undergo strong activation when the test subjects behaved bravely. Based on this finding, there is reason to assume that the same area was also activated in Urpo Koponen's brain when he lay down in front of the adder with the camera in his hands, and that this area is always activated when a person decides not to let his or her fear call the shots.

According to the researchers, their test proved that the sgACC area has a key role in reducing fear reactions. According to Nili, a person can beat their fear if they manage to maintain high activity in this area.[52] However, even if this were the case, this does not yet enable us to exercise the sgACC area in the same way we strengthen our muscles. Even if the sgACC area were indeed a kind of bravery centre, not even Uri Nili knows how one would learn to regulate activity in this area. However, Nili speculated that people could practice keeping this area active for example through neurofeedback,[53] which is a method whereby a person tries to change the way his or her brain functions by carrying out certain exercises, using real time feedback from the brains, measured for example with an EEG.[54]

---

52 Nili, U., Goldberg, H., Weizman, A., Dudai, Y., "Fear Thou Not. Activity of Frontal and Temporal Circuits in Moments of Real-Life Courage." *Neuron*, Volume 66, Issue 6, 24 June 2010, 949–962.

53 It is a matter of dispute whether neurofeedback works, and one can find expensive EEG therapy devices for sale, based on questionable science and of dubious practical value. Of course, this does not mean that the method Uri Nili was referring to would not be useful in the right circumstances. What it does mean is that one should not, at least based on the above mention, buy anything.

54 Uri Nili's comments are from correspondence between us on 22 February 2014.

Darwin may have shown us the way to the heart of fear reactions, but it was Urpo Koponen who acted against his natural reactions and built tolerance to fear until that fear was gone. In terms of the research by the Weizmann institute, Urpo managed to activate that part of his brain that enabled him to give up his helmet and to hold his face still while the snake approached.

Radical exposure can remove fear in one go, but it is both wiser and less brutal to build tolerance to a source of fear little by little. Even though it might seem that Koponen jumped into the deep end of the pool without practice, in truth it was not just this one effort. After all, Koponen had already gotten to know snakes as a boy. He had filmed them for many years, moved them from place to place, investigated their behaviour, and only then (helped by his untimely nap) taken the plunge, setting his self-discipline and defence system against each other. However, it is important to remember that even though Koponen built tolerance until he was no longer afraid of snakes, it only took meeting one aggressive adder to once again make him sensitive to them. Koponen was trying to snap photos of a pregnant female. It hissed in the heather, raised its head, and attacked. Koponen was forced to drop his camera and back away from the snake. He later said that this encounter troubled him until next spring, when he managed to gradually get back the easy rapport he had previously enjoyed with the adders.

Let us address another common source of fear: public speaking. Given that mankind has been afraid of snakes from the dawn of our species, we have also been afraid of public speaking for millennia. The Roman philosopher Seneca wrote in the year 62: "For by no wisdom can natural weaknesses of the body be removed. That which is implanted and inborn can be toned down by training, but not overcome. The steadiest speaker, when before the public, often breaks into a perspiration, as if he had wearied or over-heated himself; some tremble in the knees when they rise to speak; I know of some whose teeth chatter, whose tongues falter, whose lips quiver. Training and experience can never shake off this habit; nature exerts her own power and through such a weakness makes her presence known even to the strongest."[55] Seneca appears to be right, at least if we take fear and the reactions it causes to be natural weaknesses, and at least when they become overactive at the wrong moment. Just like with Koponen, defensive mechanisms still operate in the background, even if one has built tolerance to them. They do not disappear, because they are built into us. However, you can harden and discipline this system in many different ways so that it supports what you are doing rather than messing things up by launching defensive behaviour at the wrong moment.

Social situations such as public performances include both risks and opportunities. Fear re-searcher Daniela Schiller has called it the human jungle. By this she refers to threats, which are these days mainly social rather than physical. Nevertheless, we still have a defence system built primarily to face physical threats. For those who get anxious or are unused to difficult situations, it is generally an unpleasant, unwanted experience when this system activates.[56] Even though no one has to my

---

55 Lucius Annaeus Seneca: *Moral Epistles*. Translation by Richard M. Gummere, 1917.

56 Excitement can activate even the calmest person and help him or her perform better – however, I do not focus on this thought in this book. In the end, raising one's activation level is quite simple. For example, when I feel I am not sharp or at my best, I start to think of everything that could go wrong with the situation.

knowledge died due to public speaking, people still talk about death on the stage. You can certainly lose consciousness or your reputation in front of the crowd, even if not your life. Losing face in front of others is a painful experience that sticks with you for a long time. Everyone has been in situations where they said something embarrassing, became a laughingstock or just froze at a really critical moment. Memories of these events are stored deep in the limbic system of our brains, which is to say the part that deals with our emotions.

Our brains' risk-control centre, directed by the amygdala, is responsible for making links between earlier events and present and future threatening situations. Building tolerance weakens these links, or in some cases may even alter the emotional content of the original memory.[57] This is why for example fear of speaking in public tends to decrease when you frequently engage in public speaking.[58] You can start to build tolerance for example by holding a speech in a small family event or holding a voluntary presentation at a work seminar, moving step by step to more challenging situations. According to experts, the key thing is apparently that you must never stop practicing and make sure that the steps you are taking are not too large. Moreover, the unfortunate truth is that learning to control fear is no different than learning any other skill. After all, you cannot learn a trade by stopping by the workplace once or twice a year.

---

57 I will revisit this later when I talk about Daniela Schiller's research. It can sometimes be difficult to rebrand a memory connected to stage fright, because the original memory might be inaccessible or because it is part of a much larger complex of beliefs, feelings and memories.

58 Things can stay the same or even get worse if the person with stage fright continues their avoidance behaviour, i.e., for example avoids eye contact with the public, speaks quietly or stands turned away from the crowd.

In the same way, you cannot learn to control fear reactions by making occasional visits to the world of fear. Building tolerance is stressful and unpleasant, but it is in the end a small price to pay for increasing your living space and intellectual flexibility.

4.

Uri Nili and Yadin Dudai approach the study of fear by imaging what happens in a person's brains when they defy their fear. However, their research also uncovered an interesting fact about what happens in a person's body and mind when they overcome their fear.

One of the most interesting observations they made has to do with the conflict between thoughts, feelings and the body. It seemed to be connected to whether the test subjects were able to draw the snake toward their head despite their fear. The people who managed to do so said they were still afraid, but their skin reactions showed that they were no longer sweating. Sweating is an involuntary reaction. Although the fear was still there psychologically, the body had drawn different conclusions than the mind: it no longer believed it was in danger. However, things are not quite that simple. There was another group of test subjects whose body and thoughts were also in conflict, but in the opposite manner: these test subjects said that they were no longer afraid, but their body's defence mechanism was still highly active. They also managed to pull the snake closer. However, none of those who indicated they were still afraid and whose bodies were still in a state of alarm were able to pull the snake closer.

This result seems to indicate[59] that a person starts to act bravely when his or her thoughts and natural defence mechanisms are in conflict with each other. Taken further, this may mean that you can take back control of your body when its defensive reactions are becoming active by either changing your thoughts or the activity state of your body. What remains is to learn how to do so.

5.

This may seem to be a simple question, but how do we even know why we feel the way we feel? When we weep, we are usually not surprised by the salty drops seeping from our tear ducts. We know that the tears are connected, for example, to the death of a dear pet. We generally have a more or less blind faith in that the emotions we experience are connected to our thoughts or to what is happening around us. Our feelings are real, because they seem to have a logical connection to our experiences. However, a closer look shows that this is not always the case. One important component of emotion is particularly important for conquering fear: context.

Imagine that you are walking over a rope bridge suspended over a gorge (and that you are a man, if you are not). The bridge is so flimsy that it shakes with each step. High winds blow through the gorge, making the bridge wobble, but you manage to get to the other side. Once again on solid ground, you are approached

---

59 I must emphasise that this is a very speculative idea. For example, there is always the possibility that subjects did not speak truthfully about their feelings.

by someone you find attractive. She inquires whether she can ask you a few questions, and you agree. After you answer her questions, she hands you a piece of paper with her phone number and tells you to call if you have any questions. The situation seems clear. If you found that person attractive, you might call her, perhaps without realising that the decision you just made may have had more to do with the sensation of fear you just experienced, rather than what kind of person asked you the questions. And this is indeed the case.

A key study showing how difficult it is to interpret emotions was conducted in 1974. Researchers Donald Dutton and Arthur Aron manipulated the adrenaline surge that men naturally get in frightening situations.[60] For their experiments, Dutton and Aron picked two very different bridges: one that seemed safe to cross, and another that was frightening to cross. The researchers asked an attractive female interviewer to stand at the other end of the bridge. Her task was to conduct a short interview with the men who had crossed the bridge. However, the actual focus of the study was in what came after. The female interviewer gave each man a note with her phone number, and asked them to call if they had any questions. Then the researchers waited for the calls.

Dutton and Aron's assumption was that the men who had crossed the dangerous bridge would have a higher activation level, but they also assumed that, after crossing the bridge, the men might succumb to errors of judgment due to the extra adrenalin in their systems. And this is precisely what happened. The men

---

60 Dutton, D.G., & Aron, A.P. (1974). "Some evidence for heightened sexual attraction under conditions of high anxiety." *Journal of Personality and Social Psychology*, 30(4), 510–517.

who had crossed the dangerous bridge were extremely active in phoning the interviewer. According to Dutton and Aron, this activeness is explained by the dual nature of emotions. Physical excitement and a cognitive label combined to form an interpretation of an emotion. Even though the reason why the men were in a highly activated state was due to the adrenaline in their bodies, during the interviews they interpreted this as infatuation.[61]

Feelings are a complex mixture of different elements. They are affected by sensory input from both inside and outside the body, by hormones, neurotransmitters, by the nervous system and by conscious thoughts and hunches. Separating these factors from each other requires a great deal of practice. Furthermore, it is very slow going, and slowness has apparently been a poor trait in evolution, as we tend to construct interpretations very quickly. We are able to skilfully and quickly connect changes in the activation level of our nervous system with what is happening in our mind or environment. This is called the two-factor theory of emotion, or the Schacter-Singer theory, after its founders. What this essentially means is that the physiological reactions behind our emotions are fairly similar, regardless of the actual emotions involved, and that we need cognitive processes in order to explain emotions.

What follows is that even when you think you know why you feel the way you feel, the reason might be something else entirely. Of course, few people care whether they fell in love with an interviewer after crossing a bridge for the right or the wrong

---

61 There is dispute about the validity of Dutton's and Aron's experiments, but the bleed-over of feelings and senses on a general level has been recognised in many studies. We tend to reach the simplest and most logical interpretation of the enormous information load we receive from our senses.

reason, but if the theory is correct, then everyone can benefit from a heightened activation level by simply changing the label of the emotion. It could be of enormous use for example during everyday negotiations, argumentation, public speaking and other socially tense situations.

6.

Now let us turn to the treadmill. MIT researchers Ashley Brown and Jared Curhan wanted to find out how our beliefs about ourselves sets the paradigm for how we interpret increased heart rate and sweating. And how that affects the results of negotiations. They arranged teleconference negotiations for their test subjects – with a twist. The negotiations were supposed to take place while the test subject was on a treadmill. This way Brown and Curhan could manipulate their heart rate and perspiration. Before the experiment, Brown and Curhan investigated the attitudes of test participants towards negotiations.

They carried out two experiments, with almost identical results: those who had a positive attitude toward negotiations felt that high bodily activation due to walking on the treadmill helped them in negotiations and led to a better result in negotiations with both a car dealer and a job interviewer. Those with a negative attitude toward negotiations interpreted their bodily activation as anxiety and achieved worse results.[62] High activation

---

62 Alison Brooks' research on negotiations found that worry and anxiety are detrimental in negotiations. Subjects who were caused the most anxiety and worry before negotiations got, for example, smaller profits in a teleconference than those who had not been subjected to fear. Brooks, A.W., Schweitzer, M.E., "Can Nervous

can therefore either improve or weaken one's performance depending on how one interprets increased heart rate and sweating.

Brown's and Curhan's results seem to indicate that natural excitement can be of great benefit in situations where you wish to, or where you must succeed. However, it is only beneficial if this excitement is given a positive interpretation. If not, the extra energy that a person gets in an excited state may prove to be a burden.

Many different factors indicate that interpretations play a key role in the actual effects of emotions, i.e., whether they increase or decrease your performance. Interpretations are not fixed things, but rather something that you can decide for yourself. As stated above, the physiological basis for different emotions is very similar, but the interpretation we give them may completely change our ability to perform. It can be the deciding factor in whether we get a better deal, whether we score that goal during the penalty shootout, whether we manage to find the right keys during our first piano concerto or whether we are able to crack a difficult puzzle under pressure.

Even though negative and positive activation may seem to be opposites, they are in fact surprisingly similar to each other. In terms of bodily states, they are almost identical, so moving from a negative to a positive emotion is not a big deal for your body. For that matter, it is not such a big deal for your mind either, as moving from one context or meaning to another may sometimes happen at the speed of thought. Moreover, it is easier

---

Nelly negotiate? How anxiety causes negotiators to make low first offers, exit early, and earn less profit," *Organizational Behavior and Human Decision Processes*, Volume 115, Issue 1, May 2011, 43–54.

to move from a negative to a positive interpretation than for example to calm down, according to Alison Brooks, who has studied emotions in work situations. Based on her studies, she believes that how you interpret your excitement affects not only how a tense situation, for example public speaking, feels, but also how you succeed at it.

Brooks surprised her well-meaning test subjects by putting them in tense situations. During the first test, the participants were asked to hold a speech in front of a crowd, while in another test they took part in a maths test, and in a third they had to test their limits by singing karaoke.

Brooks surprised her test subjects by having them sing Journey's Don't stop Believing in front of the rest of the group.[63] Every singer got random instructions from Brooks for his or her performance. One group was instructed to think that they were excited, while others were told that they were to feel calm, while yet others were told that they felt nervous. At the end of the experiment, Brooks combined the analysis made by the Karaoke Revolution game with the instructions she had given the performers of the surprise karaoke songs. The group who had, despite their fear, been told that they were excited got an 80% grade for correct notes, while the group who thought they were nervous only got 53%.[64]

---

63 Brooks, A.W., "Get Excited: Reappraising Pre-Performance Anxiety as Excitement," *Journal of Experimental Psychology: General*, 2013. Brooks has talked about her research for example in an article by Michael Blanding in the *Harvard Business Review* in 2013 (http://hbswk.hbs.edu/item/7335.html) as well as by Lauren Weber in the *Wall Street Journal* (http://blogs.wsj.com/atwork/2013/12/31/get-excited-the-best-way-to-conquer-a-fear-of-public-speaking).

64 There was also a group of test participants who were given no instructions efore the singing assignment. They scored between the anxious and the excited, at 69%.

Brooks' other tests led to the same results. Those who were told to interpret their emotions as excitement or who were told to order themselves to "get excited" consistently did better than the other groups. It seems that the worst thing you can do in a frightening situation is to label your high activation level as worry or fear. It trashes your ability to perform.

However, this does not by itself mean that the nervous system should be allowed to run free. This is because there is a very simple way of regulating a high heartbeat to a level where high activation helps a performance rather than ruins it.

7.

It is a little below 20 centigrade outside. The drizzling rain has ended a moment ago, and now an unbroken field of grey clouds covers the sun. I am wearing shoes two sizes too small, as well as fireproof overalls. My five-point harness squeezes me so hard against the uncomfortable seat that I can barely breathe. The visor of my helmet is open as I wait for my turn on the circuit in Jenson Button's F1 racer from 2004. The car has 750 horsepower under the hood, 150 of which have been removed so that an amateur like me can keep the car on the track. I sit low in the racing car.[65] The wheel is full of buttons and signal lights. The speedometer in the middle has been switched off, so that I will stay focused on what is happening on the track.

---

65 Mikä Häkkinen's crash at the Australian Grand Prix led to pressure on the FI to make things safer for the drivers, and particularly their heads. It felt good to know that, if I were to drive into the wall of the track, my head would be better covered than early 1990s racers.

Before the high point of the day, which is to say two rounds with the F1, the drivers are herded together. We are shown a slideshow from hell. Cars trashed while racing are shown one after the other, punctuated by the organiser's blood-chilling descriptions of the events that led to each crash.[66] On this very track, a racing car was totalled only moments earlier. The car had rolled over on the main straight and ended up in the middle of the track, between the advertising billboards. One is left feeling that the financial cost of the destruction was a lesser pain than the humiliation that followed from being unable to keep the vehicle on the track, a vehicle at the same time infinitely sophisticated and yet bristling with raw power. In any case, we are very excited.

The roar of the F1 is brutal. My ears sting as the driver in front of me takes the straight for the last time. After he is done, it is my turn. During the first round, I warm up my tires and gears, and only then press the gas pedal. I had already decided to drive as fast as I possibly could. Waiting for my turn, something surprising happens. My pulse shoots up and I feel like my blood is roaring in my ears. What makes this feeling so peculiar is that I can think of no reason why my heart is beating so hard. After all, sitting in a car should not be that hard.

It is of course now evident to me that the all day wait, the crash videos shown before driving, the F1 screaming on the track, the tight safety belts and the closed helmet, which was restricting my breathing, had together or separately activated my body's defence mechanisms. Even though I did not think that I

---

66 The fastest time in which an F1 has been trashed was at the Hungaroring in Hungary, where a driver floored the gas pedal at the entry to the pit and drove straight into a wall. Watching the video, we laughed nervously. At the same time, everyone was wondering how to drive as fast as possible, so as not to look scared, while still driving slow enough not to wind up as the next slide on that show.

was anxious, my body disagreed, and my pulse was only getting more rapid. So I did what I knew I should do, which was to slow down my breathing and to rearrange the situation in my mind. I rationalised things like this: this car is the most powerful vehicle I have ever driven, but it accelerates to 100 kilometres an hour in the same time as my motorcycle. It is unlikely that I will reach 230 kilometres an hour on this track, which is the top speed of my bike. I am safe inside the cockpit. The structure of the car can handle a collision with a wall at over 300 kilometres an hour; and for the most part, the same goes for the driver inside the cockpit. When you are driving a bike, you can easily die at 50 kilometres an hour. Evolution did not equip us with carbon fibre bodies. Even a human cannonball would not survive without a seatbelt. As I breathe calmly and think about the situation in this new light, my pulse steadies. In a moment, I feel ramped up and focused. At that moment, the track master appears in front of my face, showing his thumb with a questioning look on his face. I answer by raising my thumb, letting the engine of the car power up, and start my own rounds.[67]

It is a confusing experience. At a subconscious level, my body decides that I am in mortal danger, and launches the necessary nervous mechanisms to deal with the situation. This reaction comes as a complete surprise to me. However, for Stephen Porges, there is nothing surprising about my experiences. Porges has over 30 years experience of studying defensive mechanisms.

---

67 In the end, I felt like I became comfortable enough to drive the formula as fast as I possibly dared. With predictable results. On the last lap, in the second to last bend, I decided to switch from second to third at the end of the bend, with the pedal floored. Restricted motor or not, the F1 spun around in a nanosecond. However, in my defence, it must be said that I stayed inside the white lines, and did not wind up as another warning example on the dreaded slideshow.

He knows that, even though the ceramic brakes of a tuned up racing car may have held, the organic breaks built into me by evolution failed.

8.

"But isn't a racing car a potentially fatal vehicle?" Stephen Porges asked me.

Yes, it is.

"And it breaks the safety principle?"

This is also true.

"It is the fulfilment of a certain kind of masculine fantasy."

I do not admit this as such, but I suppose that it is true. The fantasy part seems to be a bit of a side track, but Porges is explaining my experience using an important, fear-related principle. Play requires uncertainty, and as a consequence of that, the body starts to prepare the nervous system for facing danger by heightening the activation level of the body. This is exactly the cycle that I experienced while driving the F1.

However, the playing ends quickly if the defence system takes charge. At that moment the ease of play ends, and pre-programmed survival tactics come to the surface. In practice, what launches these manoeuvres is the release of the vagal brake, also known as the nucleus ambiguous.[68] The vagal brake, when engaged, slows down the heartbeat. According to Porges' theory, "mammals release the vagal brake in the blink of an eye, when

---

68 More precisely, the vagal brake means the vagal pathways originating in the brainstem.

fight or flight requires more power from the metabolism." When the brake is released, the slow down signal to the heart is dampened, and the pulse gets quicker." If you do the reverse, i.e., engage the brake, the signal gets stronger and the pulse decreases.[69] It is crucial to understand that you can accidentally raise your foot off the brake pedal, but you can also press the brake back on. Thanks to the vagal brake, we have the ability to regulate our autonomous nerves, which are otherwise largely outside our control. The only thing you need to know is where the pedal is, and how to use it. Luckily, Porges has spent his entire academic career researching just that.

To be more precise, Porges has studied the human nervous system, focusing particularly on the vagal brake and its evolutionary history. Even though the vagal brake is spoken of in the singular, it is actually a nerve bundle involved not only in regulating the heart but also in regulating muscles involved in facial expression, listening, vocalizing, and digestion. This nerve bundle has two main branches.[70] These two branches regulate many vital functions, and play a key role in launching or stopping the fight or flight or paralysis reactions. This is the part of the nervous system that regulates vital functions, for example heartbeat, breathing and digestion.[71] In addition, the

---

69 The vagal brake regulates the heartbeat and directly affects the heart's biological pacemaker, i.e., the sinoatrial node.

70 DMNX, or the dorsal motor nucleus, and NA, or the nucleus ambiguus. The first has no myelin sheaths, and therefore messages travel more slowly, while the second does, and therefore messages travel faster. The first we have inherited from lizards (responsible for paralysis) and the second from ancient mammals (flight-fight reaction).

71 The vagal nerve has a large impact on the balance between the sympathetic and parasympathetic nervous systems.

vagal brake regulates, in cooperation with other neural nerves, the muscles of the middle ear, vocal chords, larynx, face, and in certain situations the position of the head, in particular turning one's head to face something. This all might feel very technical and distant, but the actions of the vagal brake cannot be by-passed, and we are constantly affected by its activity states. As Porges has said, in practice our central nervous system defines our life experience – in other words how you feel.

9.

When a turtle is in a threatening situation, it acts in a manner typical to reptiles – i.e., retreats into its shell and freezes. This is not a conscious reaction. The turtle does not ponder the pros and cons of various survival tactics inside its shell, or what exactly it might be feeling at that moment. Instead, the animal's central nervous system plunges its body into a state where it preserves oxygen.

Stephen Porges likes to use the example of the turtle, as he believes these kinds of tricks of the body and the connected emotions have a logical explanation. Porges has compared animal and human nervous systems, finding both similarities and differences. Let us for example look at the reaction that people tend to call "freezing."[72] According to Porges' theory, the oldest branch of the vagus is responsible for that reaction.[73] This branch harks back to the time

---

72 However, Porges dislikes this term, as he feels it is too vague. He refers to immobilisation, which he further subdivides into two parts: immobilisation due to fear, and immobilisation due to a person being completely safe, for example while breastfeeding. These two functions are completely different.

73 Although the vagal brake is primarily regulated via the newer branch.

when our ancestors were reptiles.[74] This defence mechanism never disappeared during millions of years of evolution. If fight or flight does not help, our body still retains this ancient trick. It lowers the activity of bodily functions to a low enough level that movement is no longer possible. The facial muscles lose tension, the muscles of the middle ear no longer react,[75] the heartbeat decreases, breathing slows down and the whole body enters energy saving mode, becoming immobile. In a frightening situation, blood pressure can plunge so low that a person loses consciousness. You can pass out from sheer excitement. This strategy may save your life when you are being attacked and fight or flight cannot help you defend yourself.[76] However, when the threat is social, the turtle strategy can lead to catastrophe. If you try to hold a speech while the oldest branch of the vagal brake is in power, the results are terrible. Your face turns expressionless, your gaze sets on a fixed point in nothingness, your working memory and other processes required for handling information are badly disturbed, or your head is quite simply just empty all of a sudden. In addition, the parts necessary to produce or understand speech are only working at half power. This older branch of the vagal nerve, gifted to us by a wrinkly sack of leather packed into a hard shell, is like many other gifts – both a blessing and a curse.

---

74 Creationists probably have their explanation for the vagal nerve, based on millennia of constantly avoiding the facts.

75 This is why it is hard to hear what other people are saying when you are tense, as the muscles of the middle ear are needed in particular to hear sounds at the frequency of the human voice. However, in a dangerous or life-threatening situations it is important to detect the movements of threats, i.e., low sounds.

76 As an example of this kind of situation, Porges mentions rape. When one has no other chance of rescue, the body does the smart thing, and often manages to save the victim.

The other branch of the vagal nerve is mammalian in origin. Just like the first one, it regulates defensive reactions, but instead of causing you to freeze, it makes you get a move on. This branch helps the sympathetic system by easing up on its brake effect, allowing those changes to our body necessary for fight or flight to take full effect. When the nervous system is in this kind of state, one's heartbeat quickens, pushing blood into the large muscles. These muscles use up immense amounts of oxygen and glucose when fully active. At the same time, hormones such as adrenaline and cortisol release energy pent up in the muscles and liver for use. Feeding the brain becomes completely unnecessary at this point. The system makes sure (unlike the paralysis caused by the other branch) that the brain has enough oxygen to maintain consciousness, but not for much else. There is no time for higher cognitive functions, although the visual cortex has enough fresh blood and oxygen. When in mortal peril, hearing speech is not important, so the middle ear does not need to function. What matters is survival and quick physical action.

When the situation is not threatening, our body is in a base state, where we are social, our metabolisms operate as normal, our bodies heal damage and our stress hormones are at a low level. When threatened, our bodies begin to prepare for mobilisation. Social interaction no longer matters much, the digestive system is a waste of energy and repairing cells can wait. At the same time, the level of stress hormones starts to rise, and pulse and blood pressure shoot up. Quite automatically, our body makes adjustments to all of these complicated processes when it is preparing to face danger. When this threat turns into actual and immediate danger, the body is ready to go into full gear.

Simplifying a little, one could say that for the nervous system every situation is either safe, dangerous or life-threatening. Porges calls this system, which mainly operates on a subconscious level, neuroception. This threat-analysis radar picks up various cues and hints from your environment and from inside you in order to classify possible threats.

In other words, it is clear that when I sat at the wheel of the F1, my central nervous system interpreted the situation as dangerous. From the fact that there were still thoughts in my head and I was not staring into the distance, it appears that the younger branch of the vagal nerve, the mammalian one, had started to prepare my body for fight or flight.

Porges' work shows us concrete reasons why our bodies and bodily states do not always help us in what we want to do. For historical reasons, our nervous system always assumes that all threats are physical. It has not yet evolved to answer the problems of the social jungle, where we often need every available brain cell in order to survive the situation or to handle it in the best way possible.[77] However, we do not need to satisfy ourselves simply observing the arbitrary actions of these processes, but we can instead directly affect them by using the vagal brake.

10.

Stephen Porges has had to test his theory in practice. A few years ago, he took part in a conference in Los Angeles, where

---

77 Of course, this is only the case in situations where one needs cognitive capacity. Sometimes the fact that a lot is going on in the cerebral cortex can be an obstacle. For example, a golfer might botch their swing because they are thinking and directing their performance too much.

he had to talk in front of nine hundred people. The night before his lecture, he attended a cocktail event by the organiser of the conference. The same event was also attended by a psychologist who had promised to present Porges to the conference guests the next morning. The psychologist was terrified. She said that she was nervous about introducing Porges – not just on Porges' behalf, but because she was afraid of speaking in public in front of such a huge crowd. On a moment's impulse, Porges comforted the psychologist by assuring her that there was no reason to worry and that he would fix everything before the lecture next morning. Porges said this just to calm down the psychologist, but she took it literally. Therefore, ten minutes before the beginning of the conference, she stood in front of Porges and solemnly stared at him, saying: "Right. Fix it." She was being serious.

Porges noticed that she was speaking in very short phrases. She was gasping for breath, almost hyperventilating as she spoke. Her vagal brake was completely released, and her sympathetic system threatened to destroy her upcoming performance on stage. Porges encouraged her to do something very simple: to form longer phrases and only to breathe in at the end of each phrase. The psychologist was at first unable to do this, but word by word she managed to add syllables to words and words to sentences, managing not to breathe until the end of each long sentence. The vagal brake started to hold, lowering the tension to a tolerable level – one where it would actually help, rather than hinder her performance. The presentation went brilliantly. She was relaxed, and even looked like she was enjoying speaking to the huge crowd. These days, she uses the same method to treat clients suffering from fear of public speaking.[78]

Nervous changes affect the need for oxygen and therefore the rhythm of one's breathing. What is more, this causal relationship is two way, and furthermore we can all affect our breathing. In other words, by changing our breathing we can affect our nervous system. It is therefore our most concrete and by far strongest weapon in our battle against the unpredictability of fear and its ability to take control of us.

By manipulating your breathing, you can force your nervous system into the kind of state in which a psychologist speaking to hundreds of people or a birthday boy sitting behind an F1 wheel wants to be. However, when it comes to breathing, there are two phases, only one of which helps. According to Porges, the most effective way to press the brake is to slow down your exhalations, as it is precisely through exhalation that the vagal brake most strongly affects the nervous system. When we breathe in, we temporarily block the brake from working. When the vagal brake is active, it calms down the nervous system and enables higher brain functions.[79]

---

78 I also asked him about an article about the players of Super Bowl-winning Seattle Seahawks. According to ABC News, at least 20 of the guys on the team meditate and could apparently during the game be conscious of their heartbeat and able to regulate it. However, Porges emphasised that following one's heartbeat is less important than observing one's breathing, as breathing can be used to affect heartbeat and activation level.

79 And, thank you for asking, everything went well on the track right until the last lap, when my vagal brake kicked in and I felt (incorrectly) that I was fully in control of the situation. In the second to last bend of the track, it became quite apparent that my real problems that day were not with brakes but with the gears. However, I did learn that you cannot switch from second to third in an F1 while shooting through a bend with the pedal floored. Fear-related nervous reactions affect how safe and concentrated one feels while sitting behind the wheel of a carbon fibre missile.

According to Porges, exhalations can be manipulated in many different ways: by speaking in long sentences or stretching words, by singing, playing the clarinet or other wind instruments, practicing pranayama yoga or just by breathing with long, slow exhalations.[80] It is crucial to understand that, by changing one's breathing, one change the causal relationship between nervous system and lungs. Suddenly, one's breathing is directing the nervous system, rather than the other way around.[81]

In other words, the physiological reactions launched by fear can be reversed and used as a powerful force if one is able to give a positive label to a highly activated state. However, as we well know, this is not always enough, and therefore it is important to learn how to regulate one's nervous system through exhalations. It is now time to think back to the discovery of Israeli researchers Yadin Dudai and Uri Nili that, when their body's level of activation and their thoughts were in conflict with each other, test subjects were able to draw the frightening snake closer to themselves. We might speculate whether we could use these means to cause a conflict always when desired, and thereby unleash the required courage at just the right moment.

So far, we have focused on how to keep the cost of fear as low as possible while doing something, and how fear can even help you to perform better. We started out with Urpo Koponen

---

80 In fact, in some anger management techniques the parasympathetic system is regulated through exhaling more slowly. For example, a person could count slowly to three while inhaling and slowly to six while exhaling.

81 This is of course a simplification. To go into more detail, inhalation is sympathetic activity while exhalation is parasympathetic activity. When one strengthens parasympathetic activity by exhaling more slowly, sympathetic activity becomes less pronounced, one's heartbeat slows down and other flight-and-fight-related activities subside. This is the state in which social interaction is possible.

and building tolerance. Even though tolerance is effective, one does not always need to build tolerance in front of the real thing; sometimes, well-executed practice is enough.

Grace Under Pressure

1.

When jazz legend Dizzy Gillespie decided to celebrate his 70th anniversary in 1987 by going on tour, he gave responsibility for assembling the orchestra to his protégé Jon Faddis. Faddis, who had reaped fame as a solo trumpet player and orchestra lead man, drew up a list for approval. If Gillespie approved a musician, Jon would call him and offer a spot on the tour orchestra. One of the musicians on the list was Jukka Perko, who was still a teenager at the time. Faddis and Perko had met a year before at the Pori Jazz Festival, Finland's top annual jazz event. Having compared his playing skills during the festival against the sax player in Faddis' orchestra, Perko, who had only played the saxophone for four years, came to the conclusion that he was at least as good as the professional. He asked Jyrki Kangas, the artistic director of the festival, whether he could play a piece with the orchestra. Perko had mistakenly believed that this would be part of some kind of open jamming session that anyone could participate in. Kangas and Perko trooped into the break room of the orchestra to talk to Jon Faddis. Even though the original idea had been to play one or two pieces with the orchestra, Perko ended up play-ing with Faddis for the rest of the concert. Before leaving Pori, Faddis came to talk to Perko and asked for his phone number. He promised to one day arrange something for the teenager.

Faddis kept his promise, and called Perko after getting ap-proval from Gillespie. At the time, Perko lived at a farm in the small Finnish village of Huittinen. It was in the attic of that farm that he had started his musical hobby. Perko was surprised[82] and worried by the phone call from Faddis. A chance to play in Gillespie's band was more than he had ever dreamed of. He was worried mostly for two reasons: he would be playing with the best musicians in the world, and furthermore he would need to know how to read notes during the tour, something that Perko, who had a good ear for music, had never really looked into.

Despite his fears, Perko said yes, packed his instruments and travelled for the first time abroad.[83] Dizzy Gillespie's 70th Anniversary Big Band assembled for the first time at the SIR studio in New York. With sax case in hand, Perko walked from his hotel on 48th Avenue to the studio on 25th Avenue. The whole way there, he thought about a familiar theme: fear of playing so badly that he would bring shame on himself.

<h2 style="text-align:center">2.</h2>

Jukka Perko's jazz hobby was the result of a series of coincidences. Even though he was good at sports and at school, he was not brilliant at anything. He wanted to be the best at something, which meant that he had to discover his own thing – preferably one without competition. Perko's self-esteem has never been at its best in competitive situations, so he wanted to find something where he would not have to compete. In the small town

---

82 Perko assumed that Faddis' friendship was just friendly behaviour, American small talk.

83 For a Finn, a few trips on the ferry to Sweden do not count.

of Huittinen, Perko was in a league of his own as a jazzman. The other jazz people were not competitors but rather supporters. Perko's friends had a huge jazz collection, into which Perko slowly dived. Immersion into the world of borrowed and bought jazz recordings led to Perko asking his parents to buy a saxophone for him. When his parents refused, he got the money himself by working in the battery farm in the nearby village.

Perko, who was 14 at the time, started to practice with the help of his beloved jazz recordings. The live recordings in particular were important, because with them, he was able to get a feel for how it felt to play with top musicians. He practiced for innumerable hours in the attic studio at the farm, with only one thought constantly in his head: "Mustn't play so as I'll be ashamed." Despite the fact that playing, and the state he reached by playing, were enjoyable as such (Jukka has described it as a spiritual experience and as discovering the fullness of life), he was driven to practice by internal worry. The shame was connected to other people and betraying their expectations. The assumption was always that his running score was negative, so he tried to work hard enough to at least reach zero, and get his head above the surface. Worry and fear of shame drove him to practice. He wanted to reach a level where his fears of betraying his own and others' expectations would never be realised.

One might think that the call from Jon Faddis in 1987 would have been cause for joy. However, for Perko it exceeded his wildest dreams. It was in fact something of a shock. Faddis and Gillespie had expectations. Perko was not used to this kind of pressure, as he might make a mistake or let down the expectations of these people who trusted in him. So long as he was set up against the other jazz musicians in Huittinen, he was in a league of his own. However, out there in the wide world, there were musicians who were much better than him, and now he would be directly compared to them.

His worry and fear increased. He started to practice in his attic room under steadily mounting pressure, because on tour, he would need to master the notes and playing at a top level. Perko played like crazy, and taught himself notes, songs, song elements and the structure of music. One of the pieces, *Change to Come,* ended up on the playlist for the tour. Perko broke the song into pieces and studied what it was made of. Moreover, he was not content with just practicing how to play the song on his own instrument, but also studied the parts of the other musicians. In the end, he knew how to play the song on any brass instrument, from the trumpet to the trombone.

3.

Worry and fear of shame forced Jukka Perko to practice. This is perhaps one of the reasons why fear and the use of fear are so often harnessed as tools of change. It is true that a person can be motivated by both negative and positive emotions. However, it would be a mistake to assume that negative feelings would always or even usually work like this, or that they would work predictably. Fear of failure definitely does not always lead to better preparation, but instead it often leads to the person who is afraid of failure starting to avoid situations where they think they might fail. This is due to the two-factor nature of emotions. Both positive and negative emotions can activate or lead to passivity. While one person might grow excited and practice harder, another might grow lazy and complacent. Another factor that turns fear into a difficult companion is the fact that fear is connected to neurological, hormonal and nervous processes that were originally by no means intended to improve our performance, but rather to save us from threatening situations.

For Perko, negative emotions, failure and the connected fear of shame forced him to manically practice. He used his fear in the best possible way – his fear motivated him. His fear of shame turned into a constant state of anxiety as the tour drew close, but despite the cloud hanging over all of his actions, his skills improved and he no longer had trouble reading notes. Perko's strategy aimed at preventing a threatening future event from happening. Thus, at an extreme cost in both work and emotions, he acquired the means that had in the first place put him among Gillespie and his musicians, and which in the end helped him measure up to better and better musicians on the tour. However, even when it comes to Perko, we should ask whether he could have gotten his playing skills in some other way, or at a smaller cost to his emotions. Perhaps. However, in this case fear motivated him, and long-term stress failed to ruin Perko's mental or physical health.

At the same time, Perko had, without knowing it, already been practicing since he was 14 years old in precisely the way in which studies on top level performers recommend – in other words, in a way that helps to prepare for real, high-pressure situations.

Sian Beilock, professor of psychology at the University of Chicago, has studied collapse in performance in stressful situations. Her book, Choke, features several examples of how practice under pressure can improve your performance. Whether it is playing golf or working as a police officer, people can benefit enormously from adding pressure to their practice situations. For a golf player, it could for example mean having a friend watch them putt or playing for a small stake when practicing for a competition.

In addition, Beilock claims that at least potentially top performers are different than others – different parts of their brain activate than with other people. The difference between the top golf pros and the amateurs she studied is that, with the amateurs, the parts of the brain relating to worry and anxiety were activated, whereas with the pros the areas needed for performance were activated. Even though Beilock does not directly mention image role-play or visualisation as one of those methods, there are others who do.

George Mamassis and George Doganis, researchers at Aristotle University at Thessaloniki in Greece, carried out a test with nine young tennis players on the efforts of mental exercise on playing.[84] The method included practicing five different sub-areas. Under their coaches, the young players practiced setting goals, constructive thinking, internal speech, concentration, routines, regulating over-activation and mental images. Some of these images were just of ordinary playing situations. However, these also included one special image, where the opponent manages to carry out a perfect return after the player's own top serve. These are the kinds of situations where players face the greatest risk of caving under pressure. In Mamassis'

---

84 Mamassis, G.; Doganis, G., "The Effects of a Mental Training Program on Juniors Pre-Competitive Anxiety, Self-Confidence, and Tennis Performance," *Journal of Applied Sport Psychology*, 2010.

and Doganis' test, the five players who took part in the mental exercises had better results at tennis than the four who did not.[85]

According to the researchers, practicing even under a little pressure markedly improves your ability to succeed at real-life situations. You just have to find a set of practice conditions that suit you and optimally affect your body's defence systems. This could for example be a small cash stake or a sufficiently realistic image of the real situation.

Jukka Perko seemed to have found a way of practicing that suited him by playing in front of living and past masters in the attic of his own house. In these imaginary situations, Perko either proved that he could play, or failed trying. The images were so clear that they matched the emotions he felt when playing live with Jon Faddis and Dizzy Gillespie.

Even though Jukka was not tense about playing in front of thousands of people, he was still worried because of other people, namely other musicians – as well as his own expectations. Gillespie would lead his orchestra by standing in front of the players with his back to the crowd. If a musician messed up, Gillespie would let them know what he thought with a stern glare. He followed soloists particularly closely. Anyone can imagine what it feels like to play the sax in front of the watching gaze of a living legend of jazz.

During one of the concerts of the 70th anniversary tour, Gillespie, wearing a blue leather outfit, stood right in front of Perko when he stood up to play his own solo. In situations like

---

85 This is a small sample, and indeed the study should be seen as more of an example of what psychic exercise can accomplish, rather than as scientific evidence of the method's validity.

this, Perko's long practice showed its value. Not only was he musically up to par, but he was also mentally prepared. The young musician had, after all, in his imagination been in similar situations hundreds of times. At home at Huittinen, he had played, one after another, live recordings of old classics like *Change to Come*, *The Champ*, *Jessica's Birthday* and *Toccata*. Perko played solo sections from the same pieces during Gillespie's tour. Once Perko's solo ended, he sat down and glanced at the master, who made an approving face. The teenager answered with two bows in Gillespie's direction.

4.

At no point during the tour did Jukka Perko actually enjoy playing in Dizzy Gillespie's band. He was worried all the time. "It was just the way I was made," Perko said. Criteria set by himself, other players and the jazz crowd drained his energy, and despite a few short glimmers, Perko had got the most out of playing while on his own in the attic. "All I wanted to do was get from a negative score to zero. After that – I had no plans." Playing in Gillespie's band exceeded his wildest expectations.

It is quite natural from the point of view of this mental landscape that, even though Jon Faddis complimented Perko after a few gigs, it did not have much effect. Faddis was happy about how well Jukka had performed, and how the other musicians were giving the young sax player respect. However, that did not take away the worry. After one exceptionally good evening, when one of Perko's solos had gone particularly well, he heard a knock on his dressing room door. He opened the door to find himself facing Dizzy Gillespie. The master himself complimented Perko's playing. He may have expected Perko to be pleased at this feedback, but instead the young man started to analyse his playing: there had been one wrong note in the B section. Gillespie interrupted this analysis, and told Perko that when he comes to give the young man a compliment, Perko's part is to say thank you.

These days, Perko believes that even though worry drove him to practice,[86] the same emotion kept him from playing at his highest possible level. There were many good moments during the tour, but Perko feels that he could have gotten rid of trying too hard, if he could have let go of his worry and fear of shame. He describes this delicate interplay between rigid preparation and the idea of letting go through the metaphor of jumping hurdles with a horse. During practice, the rider gives the orders and maybe even pushes the horse to do something. But in a competition, the rider's job is to bring the horse to the hurdle and to let it jump. It is exactly the same with music, and in fact everything else. Fear and worry can increase your motivation to practice,[87] but when it is time for the real thing, fear and worry tax your ability to perform.[88]

---

86 And possibly helped him to perform at a high level in the critical situations he later found himself in.

87 Of course, even in such a case it may result in great physical and psychic harm to your health due to constant stress.

88 Jukka Perko's story is based on an interview with him on 11 April 2014. The description of Perko's solo and Gillespie's way of conducting is based on YouTube clips from the tour, for example at: https://www.youtube.com/watch?v=sS-Bq7yGnK7g

5.

In almost every area of our lives, we are measured and then judged based on those measurements. From sports to workplace to school, we are evaluated based on our performances. That is not to say that your potential doesn't matter, but eventually the performances a person is capable of during practice (or outside competitions) do not mean much. They may of course offer hope for the future, but regardless of whether we are speaking about work, top sports or art –which is to say all of the competitive sides of life – only those performances count that are undertaken when there are stakes on the table. Which is to say making it through a playoff round, winning the final or bouncing back from defeat. Or when you have to do well at a math test, university entrance examination, or job interview for your dream job. Or when a client is considering whether to complain or when you have to convince a group of reluctant listeners about something important. These are times when you are under a lot of pressure, and stand to win or lose a great deal.

Those who are the best in the world during rehearsals, on paper, or in the office, are promises, and only some of these promises can deliver their best performances in circumstances where fear, worry, over-excitement and enormous pressure are messing things up. Real ability equals the performance you are able to deliver in the real situation. Consequently, practicing under pressure, even if it is only imaginary pressure, is incredibly important and useful. It may sometimes make rehearsals uncomfortable, but it prepares you for situations where your performance is seriously hindered by fear and worry.

Fear is a sly feeling, because it tends to give false instructions.[89] Fear of failure may turn a student into an underachiever: she drops out of courses and avoids situations where the risk of failure is too great. Or she may be so worried about tests that she is unable to answer questions at the level one might expect from one of her intelligence and memory. American Buddhist nun Pema Chödrön has adopted fear as one of the main subjects of her teachings, having written books and given numerous lectures on how fear leads us astray. In one of her writings on fear, Chödrön aptly describes the mechanisms of fear and how to defeat fear through an allegorical story. In this story, a young female warrior is told by her teacher to fight fear. Despite her objections, she finds herself on the battlefield with fear. Thinking back to the instructions given by her teacher, the warrior approaches fear, bows to it (three times, touching her face to the ground) and asks for permission to fight fear. Fear thanks her for the respect she has shown. Next, the warrior asks fear how it could be defeated. According to Chödrön's story, fear replies: "My weapons are merely that I speak quickly and come right up to your face. That makes you lose your confidence and do everything that I tell you. If you don't do what I say, I will lose my power."

There is much in Chödrön's story from which we can learn. However, at the same time we should remember that sometimes it is best to do as fear tells you to do. For example, if we return to the student in the example above, fear can motivate her to spend

---

89 There are many exceptions of course, when fear gives you exactly the instructions to ensure survival or to avoid danger.

a few extra hours with her exam books, to look for answers in more than one source and to practice her exam answers. For Jukka Perko, fear was a source of energy and motivation (though we can, again, ask at what cost). Perko was keen on rehearsing mostly due to fear, and he harnessed fear as a force for good by practicing with it.[90] Practicing under pressure helped him to manage the pressure during actual performances, and while on stage, Perko was able to enter his "own bubble" with the music. His method of practicing may have been a key factor in why he was able to succeed while under Gillespie's critical stare.

However, fear could have led to Perko refusing Faddis' invitation. While on tour, fear made him wary, and according to Perko it no longer helped him. The vocabulary of fear does not seem to understand imperatives like listen, immerse yourself and let go.

In fact, what appears to be central to the cost of fear is how well one learns to make a distinction between situations where fear guides us in the right direction and where it misleads us. When does fear motivate us to rehearse, to raise our activation level or to help make sense of things? And when does it ruin our cognitive capacity, mess up our fine motor skills, mix up our thoughts and drive us to avoid situations that could be useful for improving our own quality of life or to reach our goals?

Fear brings with it something else, the cost of which is considerable: stress. Acute stress is a good thing. However, prolonged,

____

90 Of course, Perko also loved (and still loves) to play and to test his limits as a musician.

chronic stress is extremely detrimental for both your physical and mental ability. You can succeed by having a great deal of stress hormones in your system, but the price can be hard to predict.[91] However, it is not always the future that causes fear. It can also be the past.

91 One way to break out of a stressed state could be to try one's best to turn a tough situation into a game or a learning situation. According to the theories of Stephen Porges, one could turn a dangerous situation into a game, if one feels that one is in control of an uncertain situation. The defence system starts to calm down once the higher brain functions signal the all clear. This can be done for example by lowering the stakes. Another way to turn chronic stress into moments of acute stress is to find one's own way to stop worrying, i.e., to take a vacation from fear. This can be done in many ways, which all have one thing in common: to stop thinking about the source of fear. Good ways to do this include sports, play, games, meditation and in some circumstances entertainment.

A Living Archive

1.

John Marzluff, professor at the University of Washington, has studied the ravens living in the Seattle area for years. When the grey-haired professor walks in the Freeway Park wearing his green shirt and beige pants, the ravens perch serenely in the trees. However, things change when Marzluff stops, takes a rubber mask from his pocket and puts it on. Now he looks like a serial killer from a B-class horror movie, and the ravens seem to go crazy. The air is full of cawing, and the bravest carry out fake attacks against Marzluff.

This may seem strange, but Marzluff actually knew that this would happen, as he had worn a similar mask when catching the ravens. The ravens had learned to be afraid of the mask, as a man wearing that mask had hurt them and their fellows. Recognising the mask is, at least from the perspective of the ravens, a matter of life and death.

This example gives a good idea of how the primitive amygdala works. When a raven or a human being encounters a threatening situation, the amygdala makes sure that the association connected to the fear memory is retained. Using that memory, the person – or raven – can react in a blink of the eye to the same threat in the future, without the need for conscious thought.[92]

The research group led by Marzluff has also imaged the birds' brains using in vivo imaging at the precise moment the ravens are shown the dreaded rubber mask. According to the researchers, the frightening face activates the same areas in the ravens' brains as in those of people: the amygdala, the thalamus and the brain steam. Of the above, the amygdala is connected to fear memory-related associations, the thalamus to visual impulses and the brain stem to preparing the nervous system to face a threatening situation. We know that these same areas are connected with emotions, motivations and fear-related learning through conditioning.

We do not need to be taught to fear something. Like with the ravens, the fear-related mechanisms of human beings are innate. However, we do learn something – what to be afraid of. Quite often, we learn to be afraid of things that we really should be afraid of, while at times we become afraid of things that seem less sensible. Furthermore, the level of our fear is often out of proportion with the actual danger inherent in a given situation. After fear memories have been formed, they are hard to change. One can get a good grasp of how effective and stubborn fear memories can be by looking at animals. And when fear-based associations are triggered, they can be overwhelming. Just like

---

92 What is more, even those ravens that had no personal experience of the masked man reacted to Marzluff when he walked through the park with the mask on his face. Even birds that lived several kilometres away reacted strongly. What is more yet, their descendants also learned to avoid the masked man. In other words, fear spreads from raven to raven even over distances and generations.

the Freeway Park ravens going crazy when they spot Professor Marzluff with his mask.

The best strategy would be to extinguish fear memories before they are consolidated. The best person to show how that is done is probably Dr. Daniela Schiller, the acclaimed fear memory researcher, who found out how to use the vulnerability of our memory in countering fear.

2.

Riding is a dangerous sport. It is the only sport where people die every year.[93] Almost everyone who has been doing it for a while has at one time or another fallen off a horse. This also goes for my acquaintance, whose career was in effect destroyed when she fell off her horse.

As a young woman who was very serious about hurdling, she found herself riding a horse that needed to be encouraged to perform. She did not like it. She preferred horses that would charge on. However, there was something about her gestures and movements that made the horse nervous. Perhaps it was how she would nervously wave at the horse when she approached, or perhaps the horse could sense the nervousness in the way its

---

93 For example, according to the BBC, 10 riders die in Britain every year. In 2009, Professor David Nutt caused a stir when he claimed that riding is for example more dangerous than ecstasy (the drug). From this perspective, it is a little amusing to watch people try to ban MMA on the basis that it would be a dangerous sport. Of course, plaque does accumulate in the brains due to strikes and kicks, which may cause problems later on, but at least no one dies on an annual basis. However, I have heard no one suggest a ban on riding – nor am I doing so, but it is one example of how erroneously we assess real risks. We rely on our feelings.

rider guided it. Nevertheless, she was able to make the horse trot to the hurdle, but at that point the animal stopped as if it had hit an invisible wall. The young rider was hurled from its back. Hitting the ground, she felt a sharp pain in her hand – it was broken. The crippling pain left her crying on the ground, cradling her shattered hand. After that, she could not ride for a long time, and during that time, fear set into her mind. Even now, decades later, she is so afraid of taking the hurdles with a horse that she very rarely practices hurdling: "It left me with a permanent fear." When she rides, she still feels that blockage from long ago. It is of course clear that this blockage is particularly strong with horses that need to be chivvied in order to get them to move. My acquaintance developed a strong fear memory from that one event.

What most riders will tell you is that "You need to get back on the horse as soon as possible." Even though a broken bone stopped my acquaintance from doing so, she agrees with that statement.

3.

"Telling riders to get back on the horse as soon as possible after an accident is in fact, scientifically speaking, very good advice." So says Daniela Schiller, leading neuroscientist at Schiller laboratory at Mount Sinai University. The laboratory has, incidentally, been named after her. I told her the advice given to all new riders, as I believed that Schiller would be just the woman to confirm whether it actually worked. She is the scientist who proved in 2009 that fear memories could be altered without medication.

Daniela Schiller is interested in human fears. She wanted to tackle that mechanism of the brain that unravels fear memories ingrained deep in the various layers of a person's brain, in such a way that the fear does not return to disrupt their life. Fear and fear memories are an important theme for Schiller – and not just academically. Her father survived the Nazi holocaust. Despite Schiller's efforts, her father always refused to discuss his memories. She has deduced that the Germans did something to her father that he does not want to revisit. Schiller believes that this experience, of being the child of a holocaust survivor may have been a sub-conscious motive for her work. Her childhood in Israel was surrounded by fear and drama. There is another, more practical reason: fear is such a strong emotion that it is easy to measure and study. Fear is a key survival method, and the brain almost seems to be specialised in storing fear memories and in detecting and processing various threat-related signals.

4.

Daniela Schiller says that she became interested in how an individual event can take over a person's entire life. She seems to be somewhat bothered by popular ideas about emotions. "It's like we believe that people have no free will. As if our emotions were given to us from above," Schiller says. It is hard for her to accept that people seem to just passively submit to their emotions, because it is crystal clear for her that fear memories can be changed. This is due to a vulnerability in the way memories work, one which Schiller has found a way of manipulating in her experiments.

Schiller started to study whether the mechanism for organising the memory could be manipulated in order to change fear memories.[94] Despite what we may think based on everyday experience, memories are not permanent, nor can their contents necessarily be trusted. Every time a memory is brought back to mind, it must be re-recorded. Schiller compares the memory to a computer's word processor. The memory is like a file that we open, but instead of reading notes written earlier, we may end up making changes to it. We can add or remove things. When we slide down the menu and select save, the document is saved over the previous one carrying the same name – but now new data has been added. This vulnerability in our memories has been manipulated by Schiller in order to "permanently alter the frightening qualities of a memory."[95] To put it more scientifically, this operating principle of the memory is called reconsolidation.

Schiller's research group included her closest colleagues Marie Monfils, Joseph Ledoux and Elizabeth Phelps. They collected a group of volunteers for some laboratory tests. In a Pavlov-like test, the subjects looked on as squares of different colour appeared on the screen of a computer. There were two squares, but the test subjects only grew afraid of one of them, the yellow square. It was not the shape or colour of the square that frightened them, but the fact that they were administered

---

94 Schiller's test is based on an earlier test with laboratory rats, where the conditioned fear of the rats, accomplished using Pavlovian methods, disappeared, after they were repeatedly exposed to the stimulus that had originally caused their fear, with the result that nothing bad happened to them. However, only some rats lost their fear, i.e., the ones who were exposed during the time period that Schiller calls the "reconsolidation window."

95 Schiller, D., Monfils, M.H., Raio, C.M., Johnson, D.C., Ledoux, J., Phelps, E.A. "Preventing the return of fear in humans using reconsolidation update mechanisms," 2009. Nature 463, 7 January 2010, 49–53.

a painful electric shock each time they were shown the square. Each time the yellow square popped up, electrodes fixed to their wrists shocked the test subject with an electric current. Finally, again consistent with the views of Ivan Pavlov, it was no longer necessary to administer electric shocks to the test subjects, as merely seeing the yellow square was enough. Voilá! Schiller and her colleagues had implanted the fear memories into the brains of the test subjects.[96]

After a fear memory has been implanted with enough electric shocks, our old friend the amygdala ensures that the test participants will also in the future be afraid of the yellow square. However, the actual reaction takes place elsewhere. The amygdala merely ensures that the yellow square is associated with danger. This is how people learn to be afraid. However, the amygdala does not operate in a void, as the prefrontal cortex can suppress its activity. However, the prefrontal cortex does not, unfortunately, often have time to engage before the reaction is in full swing. Even though the amygdala is activated also by other sensory input than danger, the amygdala is, according to Schiller, very active in almost all of the various anxiety disorders.[97]

However, as we saw earlier, Schiller was interested in how to remove this kind of painful memory. The test subjects returned to the laboratory the next day. The researchers attacked their fear memories using a method called extinction training. Using

---

96 Two small sensors were fixed with black strings to two fingers of the off hand (i.e., the hand to which electrodes were not fastened) of test participants. The sensors were set to pick up changes in the functioning of sweat glands, which tend to go crazy when a person is afraid. In this way, the researchers were able to objectively state whether a person had undergone a fear reaction or not.

97 Daniela Schiller's comments are based on an interview with her on 11 February 2014.

that method, test subjects who have earlier been given electric shocks are repeatedly shown the same yellow square that they were taught to fear the previous day. However, this time there are no electric shocks. According to the theory, a person will gradually learn that the yellow square is not actually dangerous. However, Schiller and her colleagues knew that the test subjects would quite probably form two memories. They had the fear memory from the earlier day, and now they had a new memory of a yellow square that they did not need to be afraid of. In normal circumstances, these memories compete with each other, but are nevertheless both retained by the brain. Schiller wanted to get to grips with the actual fear memory, rather than just creating a competing memory. Even though the competing memory is usually, in normal circumstances, stronger, stress can change things so that the original fear memory surfaces easily. It comes back to bother you at the moment when your mental reserves are already weakened. Any experience that is sufficiently powerful and is connected to a strong feeling of fear is etched deep into the mind, and the amygdala makes sure that we behave in the "right" way when danger strikes. However, this is not necessarily a good model of behaviour. For example, if a fear memory is connected to failure, the defensive reactions might lead to an even greater blockage.

The researchers at Schiller's laboratory have looked for a way to address the original fear memory, which is to say fear of the yellow square.[98] In order to do so, Schiller and her colleagues

---

98 The mechanism studied by Schiller had been discovered earlier, but only through using medication. Schiller presented a method whereby fear memories could be changed using natural methods.

divided the test subjects into three different groups.[99] The first group looked repeatedly at the yellow square appearing on the screen. The members of the group received one more electric shock when viewing the yellow square, and were then allowed to take a six hour break. The third group were also given an electric shock when viewing the yellow square, but only a ten minute break, after which they were repeatedly bombarded with the yellow square. According to the theory, the original fear memory could only be tackled if the memory was brought back to mind and then changed during a certain period of time. By combining the yellow square and the electric shock, the researchers hoped to open this window of opportunity. According to Schiller, the researchers are still unsure about how long precisely this window of opportunity for changing memories stays open, but it is certainly a few hours, although less than six.

The high point of the test came the next day. All participants were invited back to the laboratory, to face a by now familiar combination. Sensors were fixed to their wrists, and they were asked to sit in front of a screen, and shown a yellow square. The sensors, which measured the conductivity of their skin, told the researchers what had happened to the fear memory. Two groups were still afraid of the yellow square: the group who had not been shocked before starting the extinction training, and the group whose extinction training had started six hours after retrieving the memory. Those who had started extinction training ten minutes after being shocked were no longer afraid. The yellow square caused no reaction whatsoever with them.

---

99 Test subjects did not, naturally enough, know about this division.

However, there were stranger things to come. Some test participants were called back about a year after the original tests, to see whether the changes could still be seen. Those who had received extinction training after the window of opportunity had closed still reacted to the yellow square. However, those who had received therapy inside the window of opportunity reacted to the yellow square as one normally reacts to a yellow square. Which is to say not at all.

Schiller and her colleagues had found convincing proof that fear memories could be changed.[100] Even better, they had shown that you did not need drugs to alter fear memories, but could use a perfectly natural method.

5.

Daniela Schiller also agreed to consider how to address fear when the original event that caused it has been forgotten. For example, childhood events cannot necessarily be recalled, but the connected fear associations still exist. According to Schiller, we can assume[101] that sometimes it is enough merely to recall the feeling associated with the memory and to try and connect a new meaning to it.

---

100 Tests indicate that this window exists, and that the original memory can be altered. Or, as Schiller reminds us, it is enough to change the emotional content of the memory. In other words, we do not need to entirely remove unpleasant memories like in Beautiful Mind, but we can instead focus on the fear attached to the memory. "When we speak about the memory, we are generally speaking about the content of a memory, while the reconsolidation window appears to be connected to the emotion connected to the memory," as Schiller told me.

101 Schiller does not claim that this is the case, but rather that one can theoretically assume this to be the case in certain situations. One must remember that she is a scientist.

The cognitive behavioural therapy mentioned by Schiller is already being used to treat people with overactive fear reactions. For example, exposure therapy can be used with people suffering from phobias. Exposure therapy means putting the patent in a situation where he or she can face the source of fear several times in safe circumstances. In situations where the fear is extremely powerful, the exposure happens on the level of images. Another way to do it is counter-conditioning. In this form of therapy, the patient is exposed to the source of fear, but before that he or she is taught various relaxation techniques. The idea is to proceed in the hierarchy of sources of fear from the least to the most frightening thing, until the patent has learned to cope with all sources of fear by relaxing. With all of these examples, the original fear memory surfaces in one way or the other, and the window of opportunity for shaping the memory is opened.

The Threat from Inside

1.

In 1933, with the gracious help of the Nazis, a group of German university students burned over 25,000 books at the Opernplatz in Berlin.[102] Famous scientific, artistic and philosophical works were cast into the flames. Documentaries and books concerning the book burnings tend to repeat the names of Albert Einstein, Sigmund Freud, Ernest Hemingway and even Jack London. What is less remarked upon is that two out of every five works burnt at the Opernplatz came from the same place: the Institute of Sexology and Sexual Medicine in Berlin.[103] Just as foreign and Jewish artists and thinkers represented the external threat to Germanness, those 10,000 books represented the internal threat.

On 6 May, a few days before the book burnings, university students stood in a row in front of a building at Beethovenstrasse 3 and carried over 20,000 books and studies as well as a collection of thousands of photographs out of it. Inside that building was the Institute of Sexology and Sexual Medicine,[104] led by Magnus Hirschfeld. A brass band set the tune as these apparently unGerman materials were loaded into a lorry parked in front of

---

102 Meanwhile, books were burned in 34 areas, all of them university towns.

103 For sources on this topic, see for example Romeo Vitelli: http://drvitelli. typepad.com/providentia/2007/08/burning-the-l-1.html, as well as Robert Biedron and Joachim Neander: http://en.auschwitz.org/h/index.php?option=com_content&task=view&id=31&Itemid=3

104 Institut für Sexualwissenschaft

the main entrance to the building, and then driven to Opernplatz for the burning.

The Institute, founded in 1919, was tasked with gathering information about human sexuality. The founders of the Institute had defined, as core research areas, contraception and sexual diseases. However, through the Institute, the founders also fought for human rights, in particular for equality of women and for granting homosexuals equal citizenship rights and equal treatment.

However, the National Socialist Party did not support the values of the Institute. Sexuality, particularly homosexuality, was such a great threat to Germanness that they had to be destroyed. As the moderate wing of the party lost power and as policies tightened, Heinrich Himmler, who had previously avoided strong statements, started a public persecution of homosexuals, and indeed declared homosexuality to be illegal. The Nazis prohibited gay organisations in 1933. At the same time, they also prohibited the scientific study of homosexuality. The police started to round up homosexuals.

Even though most of the material stolen from the Institute of Sexology and Sexual Medicine – even the bust of the Institute's director – was burned at Opernplatz, the Nazis did not destroy everything. At the Opera Square, backlit by the roaring flames, Propaganda Minister Joseph Goebels (who had a strong connection to the Nazi student association) lectured in a booming voice about Germanness and the need to purify it: "No to moral degeneration and decay. Yes to virtue and chastity in families and in the state."[105] Now the Nazis had detailed information on where

---

105 Source: http://www.ushmm.org/wlc/en/article.php?ModuleId=10005852

to begin purging moral degeneration. When they seized the collections of the Institute, the Nazis also got hold of the names and addresses of thousands of the Institute's patients.

According to a study by Rudiger Lautmann, over 50,000 men were sentenced for homosexuality. Depending on the estimate, from 5,000 to 15,000 homosexuals were murdered in the concentration camps. There is no doubt that the Jews were the Nazis' prime target, but according to the statistics, a proportionally greater number of homosexuals died. Homosexuals, identified by pink triangles pinned to their prison clothes, were beaten up and used for target practice. A man with a pink triangle was not even safe from other prisoners; many were beaten just for being gay.

As the Nazis annexed or conquered country after country, the Europe of the 1930s and 40s was hell for almost everyone who was not a part of the Aryan master race, but even belonging to this imaginary higher race could not save gays, as Nazis exposed as homosexuals were also murdered.

2.

On 3 February 1952, Alan Turing stepped into Wilmslow police station at Cheshire in England to report a crime. There had been a breakin at his house in January. It was supposed to be an open-and-shut case. Turing knew what had been stolen, when the breakin had happened, and who was responsible. All the police needed to do was to arrest the criminal and return the stolen property. However, as a result of Turing's visit to the station, the detectives were drawn to investigate a different crime. They decided to catch Turing in the act. Detectives Wills and Rimmer turned up at Turing's door without warning and told him that – allegedly – they knew that Turing had not told the whole truth about how he had discovered the thief's name. Turing was no good at lying, and after he was found out told them more than he should have. Turing even wrote a statement of several pages, one which the investigators praised as exceptionally well written. Turing knew the robber's name, because he was the acquaintance of his friend Arnold Murray. Alan Turing had had an affair with Murray, and Turing confessed as much to the police. Back in 1952, that meant that he had just confessed to a crime.[106]

Turing was not just anyone. He was an acclaimed mathematician, and the man who had built the first modern computer, the Turing machine. He is also now considered to be the father of artificial intelligence. In the 1930s, as the Nazis hunted homosexuals and other minorities in Germany, Alan Turing was studying at King's College and wrestling with the kinds of mathematical problems that were to prove decisive in the later development of computers. When World War II broke out, the British government established Bletchley Park as the UK centre for crypto-analysis. This centre, located at an old manor, housed the best minds of the country in order to search for a scientific solution to how the war could be won. And what is more, they found one.

For warfare, intelligence is key. It is needed in order to discover, and thwart the enemy's plans. One way to find out what the enemy intends to do is signals intelligence. Capturing enemy

---

106 The details relating to Alan Turing's arrest are from the brilliant biography by Andrew Hodges: *Alan Turing: The Enigma, 1992.*

signals is, by itself, simple, but as those who send signals are also aware of this, they tend to take all means possible to avoid decryption of their signals. The Germans used the Enigma device designed by Arthur Scherbius to encrypt their signals. Scherbius had already designed the device during the First World War, but it only become crucial for war during World War II. Messages to be encrypted were written using an Enigma device, which changed the characters used in the message according to a specific system. The message could only be decrypted by being fed into a second Enigma device. However, Polish scientists[107] had already broken the Enigma code in 1932, and shared their information with the Brits in 1939. The problem was that the devices had been further developed, and this old information was no longer useful by itself.[108] While working at Bletchley Park, Turing succeeded at a crucial moment. His ideas and models led to a new breakthrough in decrypting the Enigma code. Even though it is true that people often do not give enough credit to the Poles in breaking the Enigma code, it is still likely that Turing was crucial for the Second World War not lasting longer than it did.[109] The breaking of the Enigma code gave the Allies detailed information about the locations of German U

---

107 The Poles have tried to get the code-breakers some well-earned recognition. The Polish government's latest effort was an attempt in 2012 to publicise the breaking of the Enigma code by Marian Rejewski, Jerzy Rozyck and Henryk Zygalski in 1932.

108 For example, Laurence Peter of the BBC has written on the subject, emphasising that after the Second World War started the Germans changed their Enigma machines, and therefore more resources were needed to crack the codes. That is where Alan Turing's genius came in.

109 Many articles on Turing mention an estimate that the war was shortened by several years due to his efforts, without mentioning any real sources or models to prove this.

boats, changing the balance of power in the war. According to Winston Churchill, Turing played a decisive role, and Captain Jerry Roberts, who had worked with Turing at Bletchley Park, believed that without Turing, Britain would have lost the war.

However, war time heroics did not help Turing. It was 1952, and according to British law homosexuality was a crime. Turing became a suspect, then the accused, and finally a man sentenced. However, thanks to the colleagues and friends of Turing who testified as to his character, Turing was not sent straight to prison. The court allowed Turing to choose how he would be punished. The alternatives were a year's prison sentence or chemical castration. Turing chose the latter.

This meant, in practice, that Turing's libido was extinguished with a shot of oestrogen. The sentence also affected his life in many ways. As a sentenced felon, Turing had no business in the United States, and the secret service made sure that he could not return to his job. Turing was considered to be a security risk, just like all other homosexuals after two secret service agents had been exposed as double agents. A foreign power had blackmailed them with threats of revealing them as homosexuals.

After being sentenced, Turing's life slowly fell of the rails. Two years later, on 7 June 1954, his housekeeper found him dead in his bed. On the floor was a half eaten apple and there was cyanide on the table. The case was officially deemed to be suicide.

3.

Germany, which had not repealed the Nazi-enacted laws banning homosexuality, only apologised for the treatment of sexual minorities as late as 2002.[110] It took Britain longer than that, as the government's official apology was only published on 10 September 2009 in the *Telegraph*. It took several petitions and a public address, but finally Gordon Brown, then Prime Minister of the UK, wrote that he was proud to be finally able to apologise to a true war hero. According to Brown, Britain's debt of gratitude to Turing for how he affected the way the Second World War ended makes Turing's treatment particularly appalling. Instead of a thankyou, Turing was castrated, disgraced and shut outside society.

According to Brown, Turing was correctly sentenced in accordance with the law in force at the time, and the clocks could not be turned back. Nevertheless, the sentences given to Turing and other homosexuals were unfair and based on homophobic legislation. The Prime Minister also seemed to be apologising for that, due to these laws, millions of people who were drawn to members of the same sex had had to live in fear of being sentenced. Even though the government or Parliament were unable to gather enough support to overturn the sentence, Turing was in the end pardoned. Queen Elizabeth II signed a royal pardon on 24 December 2013.

These two cases give a good picture of the recent history of gay persecution. No matter which side their government was fighting for, homosexuals had to live in fear of being exposed. In Germany, those who were found out were sent to death camps, while in the UK the courts sent them to prison.

----

110 Based on the letter of the law, both West and East Germany were convinced that the Nazi German laws were just. Both countries preserved these laws in their own legislation. Hitler went, but the attitudes remained.

Even though homosexuals no longer have nothing to fear in terms of the criminal law – at least in developed countries – fear of exposure and the cycle of humiliation and bullying that often follows being found out can still get under your skin.

4.

Asher Brown 1997-2010. Tyler Clementi 1991-2010. Seth Walsh 1997-2010. Billy Lucas 1995-2010. Brown shot himself with his father's Beretta. Clementi jumped off the George Washington Bridge. Walsh and Lucas hanged themselves, Walsh from the branch of a tree in his own backyard, Lucas in his grandfather's stables. All of the suicides happened in September 2010, and probably for the same reason: bullying, which was at times severe. The boys were being bullied due to their assumed or confirmed homosexuality. [111]

Bullying is common, and until a few years ago, was not considered serious violence. Words were seen as something less than acts. As just words. However, these boys were crushed by words. They were jeered as "faggots" and constantly ridiculed. The boys who bullied Billy Lucas told him he should kill himself.

The suicide risk for gay, lesbian and transsexual youths is two or three times higher than for others. These young people are more depressed, use more narcotics and have more absences from school than others, because they do not feel safe there. Their schoolwork suffers, and they are constantly mulling over

---

111 For example, Billy Lucas never publically expressed his sexual orientation. On the other, being called gay is hardly uncommon.

grim thoughts. According to a study conducted in California by Stephen T. Russell, 55% of those who report being bullied due to their assumed or real sexual orientation also indicate depression, 45% say that they have considered suicide, and 35% have put together a detailed plan for suicide.[112] For these young people, Alan Turing, victims of the Nazis and for countless other oppressed people the cost of fear is extreme. However, whose fear are we talking about?

5.

Penile plethysmography is an imaging method consisting of a computer, a few wires, and a program for playing video and audio material and for distinguishing changes in electric currents. The test also includes a rubber band, with mercury inside. A small electric current is directed into the mercury. If the circumference of the rubber band changes, the device will register it as a change in the electric field. This device can lead us to the sources of fear.

Henry Adams, a scholar at the University of Georgia in the US, wanted an empirical answer to a question that had been puzzling him for decades: was there any basis to the psychoanalytical theory on homophobia? Adams wanted to test for example Donald West's theory,[113] according to which homophobia is particularly prevalent when a person is superficially heterosexual, but has

---

112 Russel, S.T., McGuire, J.K., Laub, C., Manke, E., O'Shaughnessy, M., Heck, K., Calhoun, C., "Harassment in school based on actual or perceived sexual orientation: Prevalence and consequences." California Safe Schools Coalition Research Brief No. 2, 2006, San Francisco, CA: California Safe Schools Coalition.

113 Est, D.J., *Homosexuality re-examined*, 1977.

homosexual feelings and sometimes even experiences. People react to this contradiction through either aggression or panic.

The test subjects were selected from those who had registered for university research, and these candidates were then divided into categories through a set of field tests. In the first test, the subjects were asked to assess their own preferences on a seven tier scale, ranging from "completely homosexual" to "completely heterosexual." The purpose of another test was to investigate attitudes towards homosexuality, while a third was intended to discover the aggressiveness of test participants.

From among the respondents, two groups of heterosexuals emerged: those who were strongly homophobic and those who were not. Sixty-seven participants took part in the actual tests. They were brought, one by one, to a soundproofed room with an armchair. The men were then asked to set in place a rubber band that would measure the circumference of their penis. After everything was in place and the test subject was considered to be calm, the test was started. The first of the four minute samples was shown on the screen of the computer. In this sample, a man and woman had sex. After a short break, another sample was shown, in which two women had sex. After another short break, there was a third four minute sample, where two men had oral and anal sex. And then the test was over. The equipment had recorded changes in the circumference of the rubber band. It did not lie – if the circumference had grown, it meant that additional blood had flown into the penis. Though it is of course not certain why blood flows into the penis at a given time, it is safe to say that erection is usually a sign of arousal.

A few findings emerged when the results were analysed. Homophobes were no more aggressive than the other heterosexuals who had taken part in the test. However, there were differences in how penis circumference changed. In both groups, participants were aroused by the sample showing a man and a woman, as well as a woman and a woman. However, there was a difference when it came to the third film. The non-homophobic heterosexual men did not react to the film, whereas something happened in the pants of the homophobes. This different was, according to the researchers, significant. According to them, the study seems to show that those who were placed in the homophobic group, who admitted that they had negative feelings about homosexuality, were significantly more often aroused by homoerotic material than the others. This did not apply to the whole group, but to eight out of ten.[114]

Adams' study seems to strongly indicate that the reason for homophobia and the connected aggression is the homophobe's uncertainty about his own sexual orientation. Of course, the study did not prove this conclusively. Adams has indicated another possible reason for the results – anxiety can also be connected to arousal and erection. In the end, the reason for the erection is less important than the timing. When a person who identifies as heterosexual sees two men having sex and gets an erection, it may be a source of considerable confusion and anxiety.[115]

---

114 When one compares these figures with those of non homophobes, the difference becomes even clearer. Twenty percent of homophobes did not get much of an erection from watching two men have sex, while 26% had a medium reaction, and 54% a clear one. The corresponding figures for non homophobes were 66% (no reaction), 10% (minor reaction) and 24% (clear reaction). Adams, H.E., Wright Jr, L, W., Lohr, B.A., Is Homophobia Associated With Homosexual Arousal?, 1996. University of Georgia.

115 When a man who identifies as heterosexual notices changes in his penis while watching two men have sex, anxiety and confusion can naturally follow, whatever the actual reason for the reaction.

Now let us look at another theory on the roots of homophobia. Netta Weinstein and William Ryan of the University of Rochester used a very different method to approach the same topic.[116] Doctor Ryan also wanted to investigate psychoanalytic theories of the source of homophobia. His research team applied a method used to uncover subconscious prejudices in their tests. [117]There were 784 test participants from the US and Germany. According to their theory, a semantic association test would uncover contradictions between internal and external identities. Participants were shown images on a screen, and before each image there was a text on the screen, either "I" or "Other." The texts were there and gone so quickly that the participant would have had time to process them subconsciously, but not consciously. According to the theory, a person would be able to categorise a given image more quickly if, for example, a heterosexual were shown the word "I" before a picture of heterosexual relations. However, if a heterosexual person were to be shown a picture of gay sex preceded by the word "I," recognition would be slower.

Based on the tests, the researchers isolated a group of people who had self-identified very strongly as heterosexual, but who in the test were quicker to associate words or images connected to homosexuality. According to the researchers, this meant that these test subjects were on some level sexually attracted to mem-

---

116 Weinstein, N., Ryan, W.S., DeHaan, C.R., Przybylski, A.K., Legate, N., Ryan, R.M., "Parental autonomy support and discrepancies between implicit and explicit sexual identities: Dynamics of self-acceptance and defence." *Journal of Personality and Social Psychology*, Vol 102(4), Apr 2012, 815–832.

117 Using this method, for example a person who feels they are tolerant to skin colour may notice that they have hidden preferences relating to skin colour. This does not mean that they would be a closet racist, but rather that the culture or family they grew up in has led to the growth of subconscious prejudices. We all have such prejudices.

bers of their own sex. After the results were combined with the attitudes of test subjects, the researchers furthermore discovered that this same group was more likely than other test participants to support anti-homosexual laws and practices. They were willing to accept more radical punishments, and had a hostile attitude to various things connected with homosexuality. According to the researchers, this shows that at least some of the opponents of homosexuality are secretly interested in their own sex.

However, what is particularly interesting about this study is the reason why, according to the researchers, people tend to have strong views. That reason is home. According to Ryan, test participants who had a clear internal contradiction were most commonly from families where the subjects felt their parents had been controlling, less tolerant, and prejudiced toward homosexuals.

Even though one should be careful about drawing far reaching conclusions from isolated studies, the evidence seems to indicate that fear can lead to a deeply life changing, disproportionate and depressing counter-reaction, which carries an appalling cost for all parties. This fear is useless.

Homophobia is an extreme – and widespread – example of how the experience of fear turns into aggression. However, it is not an isolated example. Fear turns into aggression because it triggers a defensive reaction, which in terms of aggression means the "fight" reaction. Fear may underpin many other feelings of hatred, and in some of these other cases as well this reaction is explained through an external cause, even though it stems from deep inside the person experiencing the hatred.

6.

The suicides by the teenage boys deeply affected writer-journalist Dan Savage. He did not know the boys, but was able to place himself in their shoes, having lived through many of the same experiences. He had also been called names, bullied, and shoved. Savage and his husband Terry Miller had an idea. They sat down at a café table, put a microphone on the table, and set their video camera to record as they spoke. Their message was meant for young people, and its key message, in accordance with the title of the video, was: "It Gets Better."

On the video, Dan and Terry tell about how they were bullied at school, about how they came out and about how life got better after they stopped being teenagers. The video turned into a project that has spread to over fifty countries, and hundreds of thousands of people have taken the pledge by sending their own "it gets better" video to the project site. Many of the stories paint a picture that is at the same time sad and yet comforting. They are sad because it seems that our love and feelings can still brand us socially. Many were afraid to go to school, as every day they had to fear being bullied due to being different. Some were afraid that they would be found out under the X-ray vision of their schoolmates.

All of the stories contained a seed of hope. It seems that things really did get better. Even if you have marked a day in your calendar for suicide, thanks to a single friendly action you may cancel these plans and get a new zest for life. Other people might not look down on you after all, your family might not abandon you, and a gay man or woman is not doomed to be alone forever. As one person put it: "I have learned that sometimes my own fears about other people's reactions are in the end just my own fears, and have nothing to do with reality."[118] Here, as with so many other things, fear destroys until it is exposed.

118 This comment was actually published in a book made of "it gets better"–stories. *Kaikki muuttuu paremaksi*, Paasilinna 2010, Ibid., pseudonym P, 22 year old writer from Pori, p. 25.

No Fear so Small or Silly that It Could Not Make You Unhappy

1.

One of the great curses of modern life seems to be the endless number of choices we have. Whatever we choose, it is very likely that we would have had another, better alternative available: a better party, a more interesting experience or a more satisfying feeling of social fulfilment. If there is anything unique about our age, it is the fact that an ever increasing portion of this horn of plenty has been made visible. Communication networks enable an unprecedented mobility of information, but the social media has at the same time turned FoMO into a supervirus.

FoMO stands for Fear of Missing Out. Fear of missing out due to a choice one makes is a rather senseless phenomenon. Instead of concentrating on what is happening around us, we worry about what is happening elsewhere at the same time. This term is used particularly for the social media. Due to FoMO, one can continuously take part in the experiences of other people or get information on something better that is happening at that moment.

This draws us inevitably back to the connection between the two different definitions of fear: fear, which is caused by an immediate threat (fear proper) and fear caused by thinking about frightening things or events, which is usually called anxiety. Psychologists (usually) make a clear distinction between these two, but as we know by now, they both jump start our defence mechanisms. If a snake's head is up and it is hissing a metre from your foot, what you are experiencing is fear. On the other hand, if you are merely thinking about snakes well in advance of even entering the forest and get very uncomfortable, that is anxiety. None the less, frightening things can also sometimes be stimulating or pleasant. Fear makes us focus. A horror movie, a rollercoaster or playing an instrument in front of a crowd keep us tightly focused on the here and now. However, thinking about future events that are stressful or frightening takes our minds away from the here and now, and that's what FoMO does. When it comes to FoMO, fear (and its miserable effects) actually relate to something that you cannot even achieve. You cannot always be where the best party is happening.

Our devices cannot alleviate our anxiety, as the social media keeps us posted about those members of our own networks that are not present at that moment. It also informs us about future, potentially rewarding experiences we could participate in. This network of loose social connections has brought FoMO to the next level. There is constantly something happening on Twitter, Facebook, Instagram, Snapchat or Periscope that we should be involved in to avoid our fears coming true: had we not been near our smartphone or computer, we would not have experienced that thing we just liked or been privy to an interesting discussion.

FoMO is such a strong phenomenon that it can even be used in designing user interfaces and services, and naturally in marketing. A company called Fomomedia has posted on its Twitter feed that it can turn this ever-present fear to the advantage of its clients.[119] On its web pages, the company states that it uses digital media in order to turn event attendees into brand advocates for its clients. There is nothing wrong with this – after all, this company is doing exactly the same thing as every other firm struggling in the middle of an overabundance of products and services. One merely has to understand that modern media literacy includes understanding that a great number of well paid, intelligent and creative people are fighting and conspiring to catch our attention. They have an enormous amount of data at their disposal (yes, we constantly leave digital trails through our activities online), which helps them to make scientifically accurate observations about how to best hook users. They orchestrate a plethora of tests for a great number of participants in order to find out what captures our attention and what makes us grow attached to the services they are offering. And fear, more than anything, always sells.

Researcher Andrew Przybylski wanted to get a better grasp of FoMO through a study into who is most susceptible to FoMO and what are the consequences. Przybylski's group wanted to first of all find out how people who have fallen victim to FoMO behave. The group ended up with a battery of ten questions, based on which the severity of FoMO could be assessed in individual cases:

1. I fear others have more rewarding experiences than me.
2. I fear my friends have more rewarding experiences than me.

---

119 www.fomomedia.com: "Using digital media to turn event attendees into brand advocates."

3. I get worried when I find out my friends are having fun without me.
4. I get anxious when I don't know what my friends are up to.
5. It is important that I understand my friends' "in-jokes."
6. Sometimes, I wonder if I spend too much time keeping up with what is going on.
7. It bothers me when I miss an opportunity to meet up with friends.
8. When I have a good time it is important for me to share the details online (e.g., updating status).
9. When I miss out on a planned get-together, it bothers me.
10. When I go on vacation, I continue to keep tabs on what my friends are doing.

Participants were asked to assess their own relationship with these questions on a scale from "does not describe me" to "describes me extremely well." These questions were used to weed out the victims of FoMO from the others. People who had a constant fear of being left out seemed to have an obsessive need to use the internet to be simultaneously present in a social event happening elsewhere. They were not interested in being in contact with the people that were in the same physical space. As expected, young people were most susceptible to FoMO; it may nevertheless come as a surprise that young men were particularly vulnerable.

The researchers were interested in discovering whether these people had anything else in common besides age and sex, when examined from the perspective of motivation and self-determination theory. According to this theory, healthy self regulation and psychological health depend on three factors: autonomy, i.e., self authorship or personal initiative, competence, which is to say the ability to act purposefully, and relatedness with other people. It turns out they did have factors in common.

According to Przybylski, the FoMO phenomenon can be understood as self-regulatory limbo arising from situational or chronic deficits in psychological need satisfaction. In other words, those who are constantly afraid of missing out are more often unsatisfied with their ability to regulate their own actions and to affect their own competence. They also feel like they are more detached from other people.[120]

However, Przybylski emphasises that the connection between these two things can be created through at least two different ways. First of all, the person with FoMO may already have been unsatisfied when it comes to these psychological basic needs, and was for that reason driven to use social media. Alternatively, a person can spend a great deal of time on the social media in order to have contact with other people and to learn social skills.

According to the study, the most tangible problems created by FoMO are mental detachment from social contact in the here and now, and obviously a risk of traffic accidents. There is an up to four times greater risk of a traffic accident, if the driver is tweeting, sending emails, liking or texting while at the wheel.[121] And those with severe cases of FoMO can't seem to let go of their devices. Furthermore, although the consequences

---

120 Przybylski, A.K., Murayama, K., DeHaan, C.R., Gladwell, V., "Motivational, emotional, and behavioral correlates of fear of missing out," Computers in Human Behaviour, Volume 29, Issue 4, July 2013, 1841–1848.

121 McEvoy, S., Stevenson, M., McCartt, A., Woodward, M., Haworth, C., Palamara, P., Cercarelli, R., "Role of mobile phones in motor vehicle crashes resulting in hospital attendance: A case-crossover study," BMJ, 331, 2005 428–430. Apparently, these people never stop to weigh the pleasure of reading a friend's whinging on Facebook to the risk of accidentally driving over a school kid on the sidewalk.

on the personal level are not as lethal, according to Przybylski's sources, another costly detriment of FoMO is that we miss out on real social interaction in the here and now. While physically present, the person with FoMO's mind is elsewhere and their hand is on their smartphone. The obsessive need to be logged into the social media only heightens the feeling that we have not made the best choices in our own lives. This might make us feel bad in short term, but there may be something else at play. Just like other sources of anxiety, FoMO makes the mind wander. The anxiety and stress caused by FoMO may levy an additional personal cost: unhappiness.

2.

If we had to find just one thing with the most impact on the subjective feeling of happiness, we should talk to Matthew Killingsworth. Killingsworth, a doctoral candidate with the Daniel Gilbert Laboratory at Harvard published an app in 2009 that seemed to take the pulse of our times – and received considerable media interest. Even though the app was a little clunky and did not allow users to take pot-shots at pigs or publish selfies for all the world to see, it soon had 5,000 users. Subsequently, a total of 15,000 people from over 80 countries have participated in this giant human experiment. Killingsworth collected a total of 650,000 samples of real life experiences into his app. Most of his respondents probably want more and detailed information about how to improve subjective happiness. I am one of them.

Killingsworth, an engineer working in the software industry, left his job, and signed up at Harvard to study happiness. Perhaps because of this engineering background he was not content with just asking a few people what they felt after the fact. Instead, he decided to collect real time information from the field about human behaviour and emotions from. His app did exactly that, as it collected people's authentic experiences at the moment they happened. This method is called experience sampling.

You log into the app online.[122] Participants are first asked for background information about their life situation, personality, money affairs, professional affairs and health. After finishing the survey, the human experiment begins. Killingsworth's app sends questions according to a random schedule by either text message or email. The questions vary, but each question has the same premise: what do we do or think at the moment when we feel happy, and what we do and think when we feel blue.

Killingsworth randomly picked 2,250 people from among the first 5,000 respondents and started to feed them different questions than the rest. The app sent them questions where they were asked to tell (again, at random times) what the respondent felt like at that moment, what he or she was doing, and whether he or she was thinking of something else than what he or she was doing at the time. If so, he or she was asked whether it was pleasant, neutral or unpleasant.

The answers he got were rather surprising. What a person was doing (and whether that was something he or she wanted to do or not) did not appear to have much impact on his or her happiness. Which is to say there was an effect, but less than one might expect. Something else entirely seemed to affect people's happiness: whether their minds were wandering. When they

---

122 www.trackyourhappiness.org

were thinking about something else, people tended to report being unhappy. However, when they were focusing on what they were doing in the here and now, even if that happened to be unpleasant, for example commuting to work, people reported being happier.

It is easy to argue that Killingsworth did not account for causal links – perhaps an unhappy person tends to let his or her mind wander. Even though Killingsworth cannot entirely discount this possibility,[123] his data seems to point to a reverse causality. Going through his raw data, he tried to see whether negative moods followed wandering thoughts or the other way around. The answer seemed to be unequivocal: letting your mind wander from the now leads to feelings of unhappiness, and not the other way around. [124]

All in all, what a person was thinking seemed to better explain happiness than what they were actually doing. What exactly a person was thinking about did not seem significant. Even if a person was thinking about positive things instead of neutral or negative ones, he or she tended to be unhappier than those who were just thinking about what was happening in the here and now. Nevertheless, those who let their mind wander to negative associations were also unhappier than others.

To conclude their study, Killingsworth and Gilbert stated that the human mind tends to wander, and a wandering mind is unhappy. There is an emotional cost to the ability to think about something else than what one is currently doing.

---

123 As he states in his study, negative emotional states have been known to cause the mind to wander.

124 Killingsworth, M.A., Gilbert, D.T., *A Wandering Mind Is an Unhappy Mind*, 2010.

Based on his data, Killingsworth seems to be claiming that whenever our minds are not on what we are doing or experiencing at that particular moment, we are unhappy.

Never Try

1.

Taneli Tikka walked around his flat and talked on the phone. The 23-year-old CEO was wearing a t-shirt and underpants, his hair standing on end. He was engaged in a teleconference with his partner and the company's investor. The pressure was on. They were out of money and the company was in trouble. They decided to file for bankruptcy for the company that Tikka had founded – there was no other alternative. Each participant in the teleconference reacted in his own way. The investor fell silent and did not say another word until the call ended. Taneli still has no memory of the rest of that day.

Tikka founded a company named Taika – "magic" in English – in 1999. He had high hopes of using the company to turn the internet into a social medium. The company managed to find funding, even though the IT bubble had just burst. Tikka invested his own money, and a hefty bank loan. In addition to money, Tikka invested his most cherished ideas and all he had learned into the company. However, it was now time to kill his darling. In August 2002, the CEO was tasked with filing the application for bankruptcy with the local district court. Tikka was suddenly bankrupt and unemployed.

After submitting the application, the company was in a kind of limbo. The operational management informed the company's employees about the situation, and waited for the district court decision. It was time for everyone to wait and see. The CEO no longer had an income from the company, but the invoices were still coming in. The latest credit card bill, 4,500 euros, dropped into his letterbox. He had to pay it with his own money – he could no longer charge the company for expenses. In addition, Tikka had not collected his salary for four months, as he had stopped paying himself after things started looking bad for the company. He also had to clear out his apartment, which had been a job benefit. He carried his things out of his perfect bachelor pad, located at a prime spot in Helsinki and drove them to his new apartment in the nearby municipality of Espoo.

His new home was located in an area built in the 1970s, which provided a stark contrast to his great flat in the city centre. Tikka's studio in Helsinki had had high ceilings and huge windows with a park view. The new apartment in Espoo had a low ceiling. Where his city flat had had a sauna cabinet, he now had to manage with a tin hut in a concrete pre-fab.[125] The Espoo apartment was a dump. The cigarette smoke-stained walls were so thin that the neighbours' arguments and night time activities were fully audible in Tikka's apartment. He no longer had a car, and it felt like commuting between home and the city centre took most of his time.

Tikka weighed his situation. Who would employ a man who had gone bankrupt in his early twenties, and what would people think about him after this? Joining the foreign legion seemed like a viable option. Tikka actually had a friend who had joined the legion, and given that Tikka had served in the special forces as a

---

125 The general belief was that Värtsilä built them for pre-fab houses; ship toilets for those moving into the city.

conscript, he had a better than average chance of being accepted. As a legionnaire, he would get a new identity and nationality. Tikka figured that his debts and records of the bankruptcy would be left behind with his old personal identity number. He would get a clean slate.

The other option seemed more painful: going through with the bankruptcy, getting a new job and paying off his debts. However, this is what Tikka chose, even thought it meant giving up his dream of being a rich entrepreneur. It would also mean spending years slowly paying back his debts. He felt anxious and extremely frustrated.

Tikka vented his anxiety on an Excel spreadsheet. He broke his debt down to its component parts and started counting. How long would it take to repay the loan? How much would he need to earn in order to have money left over for rent, commuting and living? He opened up another spreadsheet, this one for what he was eating. He also worked through his anxiety with exercise. Tikka worked out several times a day: jogging, lifting weights and martial arts. Tikka, who had previously weighed over 100 kilos, lost 30 kilos during the fall and winter.

His anxiety was also reduced by working on his own values and attitudes and by finding a job. A well-paid consultant's position helped to balance his finances and kept him on track to repay the loan. But he was already thinking ahead – to founding a new company.[126]

Spring came, and as the days slowly got warmer and brighter, Tikka grew less depressed and irritable. His thinking changed. Instead of wallowing in bitterness and doubt, Tikka started to

---

126 These days, Taneli Tikka is a successful serial entrepreneur.

rethink how he felt about his bankruptcy. Going through a bankruptcy had been an excellent education in dealing with pressure and focusing on the essentials when in an extremely difficult situation. Tikka had learned a great deal about organisations and about people. He started to think that it would now be much easier to run his next company. At the same time, he grew increasingly certain that all his worries about how other people would see his bankruptcy as a failure were just wasted energy. Only seven months after the bankruptcy of Taika, Tikka resigned from his regular job and founded a new company.

The story of Taneli Tikka is a lesson in resilience. However, at its core it is more than just a clichéd "never give up" experience of the kind peddled by self help books. We can find a more interesting and useful lesson to draw from his experiences by focusing on a very specific area of Tikka's approach to failure. To get a deeper understanding of one plausible explanation of Tikka's bouncebackability, we need to carefully watch kids who are trying to solve hard puzzles.

2.

I am watching a YouTube video of an experiment organised by Professor Carol Dweck and her colleagues at Stanford University.[127] In the video, fifth graders are given a pile of blocks decorated with different colours and geometric shapes. In front of them on the table, there is a piece of cardboard with a picture printed on it. The children are asked to set the blocks in

---

127 https://www.youtube.com/watch?v=TTXrV0_3UjY

such a way that their surface forms the same picture as on the cardboard. The first tasks are easy, and all the children succeed. However, when the children finish, not all of them receive the same kind of feedback from the adult sitting on the other side of the table. When the picture is ready, some are complimented on their intelligence: "Wow, you're really smart." Others are also complimented, but in a different way: "Wow, that went really well, you must have worked so hard." The difference may seem negligible, but as the tasks are made harder and everyone has trouble finishing in the allotted time, this difference turns out to be very significant indeed.

After all the children had each in turn failed, the still-encouraging researcher gave them a chance to explain what happened. On the video, a dejected-looking little boy states that he probably had trouble because he is not very good at that kind of task. Interestingly, the most significant difference between the two groups only emerged when the researcher asked the children what kind of task they would like to do next. The children get to set the difficulty level of the jigsaw themselves. At this point, something peculiar happened. The children whose intelligence was complimented chose, almost without exception, an easier task. Those who were complimented for their hard work almost always chose a difficult jigsaw.

This experiment is based on years of research by Professor Carol Dweck of Stanford University on how thoughts and beliefs affect behaviour. Based on her work, Dweck has found that people think of ability as either something that is innate or something that is the result of hard work. The kind of thinking that Dweck calls fixed is defined by the belief that one cannot meaningfully develop one's own ability. In the experiment above, the children were guided through feedback to think that they were proving to themselves and other that they were either smart or dumb. According to Dweck, she had also fallen victim to this mindset. Dweck was always at the top of her class at school. She was perfect, so perfect that she gradually started to avoid situations that could have threatened this illusion. At sixth grade, Dweck won a spelling bee at her school, but refused to take part in a regional competition. The next year, she was the best French student at her school, but again refused when the teachers suggested that she ought to enter a competition for all French students in the city. According to Dweck, she had to let her world shrink. "Why risk it, when you're already perfect?"[128]

Dweck has carried out the experiment with hundreds of children, and in some of these experiments up to 90% of the children whose intelligence was praised chose an easy task, the one that proved that they were intelligent. However, there is also another mindset, which Carol Dweck has called the growth mind-set. A person who follows this way of thinking believes that his or her abilities can be developed through working diligently. Just like the children who received feedback on their work, an adult with this mindset is better placed to deal with failure at a task merely as feedback. Even if you do not succeed at a given task in the allotted time, it does not mean that you are stupid. You just had not learned how to solve that problem. This is just how the second group of children behaved. They stayed active and curious despite having failed. They looked on the first attempt

128 Carol Dweck has spoken of her experiences and history for example in the lecture series The School of Life; Sunday Sermons 7 July 2013. http://www.theschooloflife.com/library/videos/2013/carol-dweck-on-being-perfect/

as a learning experience, and wanted to continue doing harder jigsaws. The difference between the two groups was even more distinct when Dweck looked at how the different mindsets were visible in brain imaging.

In experiments carried out at Columbia University's laboratory, the areas of the brains relating to interest and participation were only activated with people who had a fixed mindset when someone was assessing their abilities. When the same group was given information on how to do better at the failed task, their brains did not show signs of interest in the instructions. But this was not the case with the children who had a growth mindset. Once again, those with a growth mindset proved to be completely the opposites to those with a fixed way of thinking. When they were given information on how to do better, their brains were working at full capacity.[129]

Dweck's experiments prove, for their part, that fear carries an immense cost. A talented individual can be doomed to be an underperformer, never discovering his or her latent talents due to the wrong mindset. He or she starts to fear the consequences of failure.

Dweck's experiments with the children also make us see Taneli Tikka's story in a new light. Though many people are defeated by bankruptcy and draw far-reaching conclusions about their own abilities, Tikka merely took the bankruptcy as feedback.

---

129 Carol Dweck tells about the experiment in her book *Mindset: The New Psychology of Success*, p. 18.

3.

The experiences of serial entrepreneurs like Taneli Tikka make you wonder about whether there is some essential quality that they have that allows them to turn failures into learning experiences, rather than events that breed fear that defines the choices they make for the rest of their lives.

Tikka's story about his bankruptcy and what happened next resembles Carol Dweck's children who wanted challenging jigsaws even though they had failed to solve them the first time. I asked Tikka to do a test designed by Professor Dweck to discover deep-seated attitudes on intelligence and ability. The test consists of a number of questions that are variations on the same theme. The participant has to answer whether they strongly agree, strongly disagree, or something in between with the claims made in the test. Among other claims relating to intelligence are the following:

- You have a certain amount of intelligence, and can't really do much to change it.
- You can learn new things, but you can't really change your basic intelligence.
- You can significantly develop even your innate intelligence.
- No matter who you are, you can significantly change your intelligence level.
- It doesn't matter how intelligent you are, as you can always develop your intelligence quite significantly.

After Tikka had answered all these questions, he received a straightforward answer: "You agreed zero times with the claims corresponding to the 'fixed mindset' and eight times with claims corresponding to the 'growth mindset.'" It is interesting to compare Tikka's story of his childhood coding experiments with the children in Dweck's experiments. When he was six years old, Tikka's mother gave him a Commodore 64 and an English programming manual. His next computer was an Amiga, which Tikka programmed time and again into a complete freeze-up. Hundreds of times. After each freeze-up, he would power down the computer, restart it and try again. This is a perfect example of a growth mindset.

Before entering military service, Tikka prepared for the Basic Test 1, which all new conscripts have to do.[130] Tikka studied a practice book for intelligence exams the whole train ride from his garrison in eastern Finland to Helsinki. The test was held there in a big movie theatre. At the beginning of the test, the conscripts were told that most of them would not have time to complete the test. However, Tikka managed to answer the tests during the allotted time, and even had time to review his answers. Ninety days later, the commander of the reconnaissance company asked Tikka to come speak with him, to make sure that Tikka would apply for the Reserve Officer School. Tikka had received the best scores in his intake. He worked through the tests without feeling any pressure. It was again a matter of getting feedback, rather than a harsh judgement of his intelligence. His life seems to be full of examples of a classic growth mindset.

---

130 Basic Test 1 is a test of the Finnish Defence Forces undertaken by all conscripts between the third and sixth weeks of service. It includes sections testing visual, linguistic and numeric reasoning in order to measure a conscript's overall scholastic aptitude, i.e., general ability. Stakes, http://www.stakes.info/rekisterit/ddixml/RET-KI0018.xml

It is impossible to tell where and how Tikka learned this lesson. Perhaps his parents encouraged him as a child (as Dweck's theory seems to indicate), or perhaps his early life contained a series of fortunate, random events. Who knows. What is more important is whether an adult can learn this same mindset. According to Professor Dweck, the answer is unequivocally yes. Beliefs are learned patterns of behaviour and attitudes, and deficient thoughts can be replaced with ones that work. According to Dweck, one of the greatest fears of those with a fixed mindset is that they will try but fail. One can work on this fear by first changing one's attitudes about change, growth and learning. Dweck encourages us to believe that change is possible. Ironically, we may believe that everything is based on talent even when our own past is full of examples of how we have changed or learned things that we did not know before.[131] In fact, the whole concept of changing one's mindset can be condensed into one thing: it is not always and at all times about you and proving yourself to others, but about learning. This mode of thinking takes almost all of the pressure away from high stress situations.

However, fear of failure does not stem merely from what a person thinks. Behind our thoughts and feelings there may be a genetically coded chain of events. If we study it, we can better understand the strong emotions connected with failure, and learn to avoid their unfortunate consequences, such as underperforming and giving up.

---

131 What is often essential is how one is used to learning. Those who usually learn quickly may find it difficult when they make slow progress. However, this does not necessarily mean that they would have exceeded their own natural abilities. What matters is whether their energies are spent on defending their own ego or for example on thinking of better problem solving models for their company.

<h1 style="text-align:center">4.</h1>

Markku Niemivirta, professor of behavioural science, has carried out experiments on the fear of failure at a laboratory at the University of Helsinki. His results indicate that reactions to failure and mistakes have a neurobiological basis.

Niemivirta had his test subjects take part in tests where they each ultimately fail, meanwhile observing their brains using EEG and MEG devices in order to see what happens when a person makes a mistake. The EEG unit is in the city centre, in a room that looks like the demented offspring of a hospital and an elementary school. This colourless little room, where even beige forms a contrast, has been filled with various technical measuring devices intended to ensure that the measurements are as precise and scientific as possible. The devices are operated by a technician, who ensures that test participants have no phones, metal implants or other objects that would interfere with devices measuring electric activity.

The test subject is fitted with an EEG helmet bristling with wires. With the helmet, the researchers can measure electro-magnetic phenomena in the cerebral cortex. In addition, participants' pulses and skin conductivity is measured. This combination gives a fairly accurate picture of the timing and intensity of their reactions. Niemivirta is particularly interested in whether the reactions of adults and children who are afraid of failure are different than those of people who do not have an exaggerated fear of failure.

The test is simple. The test subject has an EEG helmet on their head and sensors on their left hand. There is a screen in front of them, with large buttons. When the test begins, the test subject stares at the screen, with five images flickering in front of them: a pig, a wolf and three apples. When the wolf is pointing toward the pig, the test subject is supposed to press the right button. When the wolf is facing away from the pig, they are not supposed to press a button. The reaction should immediately follow the sequence of symbols flashing on the screen. Test subjects are also told that thinking for too long is a mistake.

The test itself is stressful for many. The symbols flash past on the screen, and even though participants fix their eyes on the screen and concentrate intensely, at some point everyone loses focus enough to make a mistake. In fact, Nimivirta's research is all about the mistakes, as when a mistake happens, the sensors on the participants' skin record the whole array of reactions relating to the mistake. When enough results have been collected, participants can easily be divided into various groups. It is easy to make distinctions between the reactions.

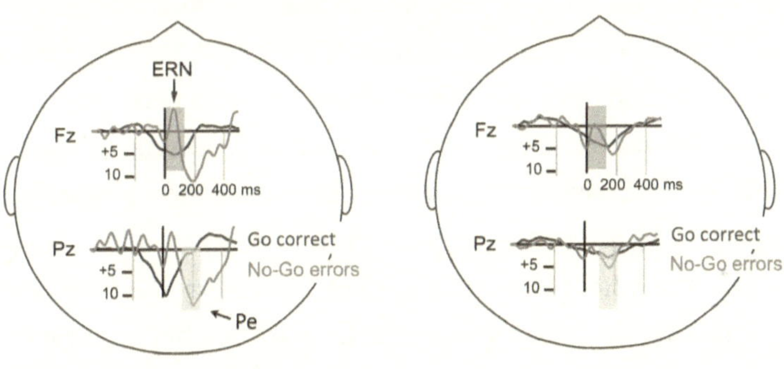

High in sensitivity to failure   **Low in sensitivity to failure**

The first reaction one can see in the EEG is recognition of the mistake. This reaction is particularly strong among those who are sensitive to failure.[132] The next strong reaction is, however, far more interesting. The second reaction recorded by the devices is the moment when a person learns that attempting a difficult thing is risky, and that one should not try anything new or difficult, because it is painful. This reaction is very difficult particularly for those who are already afraid of failure. This is an emotional reaction caused by the mistake. When observing the test subjects, one sees that the first reaction takes place in that part of the brain responsible for recognising mistakes, while the other can be detected without any equipment. When a person sensitive to mistakes feels disappointed, one can see them grimace, wrinkle their brow and swear. "Fuck" is a fairly common expression among Niemivirta's test subjects.

The second image shows a reaction typical to those persons who do not find mistakes pleasant, but also do not swear, grunt, or throw objects around the room after having pressed the wrong button. Their advantage is that, after a mistake, they are able to turn their attention, for example, to learning from the mistake, while those who react more strongly to mistakes may go into a panic. According to Niemivirta, this is the most interesting thing about his results. Those who are sensitive to mistakes detect a mistake and have the opportunity to correct their actions but often fail to do so due to the intensity of their reaction. Meanwhile, the other group, who are not shocked by their mistake, would have the capacity to correct their actions, but do not seem interested. They often have a "who cares?" attitude.

---

132 Test participants are divided beforehand into two groups: those who have unusually strong attitudes concerning failure, and those for whom failure is unpleasant but nothing to worry too much about.

The reactions do not greatly affect the number of mistakes. This quite simply means that those who are afraid of failure use an enormous amount of resources in order to reach the same result as those with a more relaxed attitude to mistakes. However, the reaction is not insignificant. According to Niemivirta's studies, being prone to reactions may have great significance particularly for a person's future. Those in the first group have more than just their EEG results in common. They have some negative habits with long-term effects in their lives. They give up more easily in the face of challenges, avoid certain kinds of tasks and environments and do badly at challenges where they have an advance expectation of weak performance. Most of those with strong reactions in the test are introverts. However, not all members of the group give up, and some may for example reach exceptional success at school – at a cost. According to Niemivirta, students who avoid failures and mistakes grow exhausted and anxious more easily than others. In addition, mistake averse students are more likely to be depressed than others. For these people, fear of failure carries a terrible cost in terms of quality of life and professional and academic success.

According to Niemivirta, what kind of reaction model a person has is genetically determined. However, this reaction model does not as such indicate that people who react strongly to mistakes are forever doomed to be self-flagellants and under-performers. Niemivirta's tests show that identical twins may have similar reactions, but still may behave differently when they make a mistake. Genetic heritage therefore determines what shows up in measurements, but not what happens after the reaction.

You cannot wish away a reaction. You just have to learn to live with it. This means that even though you may feel bad about making mistakes or taking risks, you will still get into situations where there is a risk of failure – situations where you are assessed, under high social pressure, and where you are forced to confront the limits of your own abilities. You can affect what happens after the reaction. "Many people think that they have to live with suffering for the rest of their lives. But that's not the case. Through tolerance, you can change your subjective experience," according to Niemivirta.

You might think that fear of failure is a person's private affair. However, we should not overlook the fact that it has a cost beyond the personal. The fear that gnaws on private individuals has surprising social and economic effects on society as a whole.

5.

If you, the reader, are Danish, Finnish, Australian, Colombian, Dutch or British, it is likely that you have a very positive attitude toward entrepreneurship. This is particularly the case if you are under thirty. The same goes for most of the world, except if you are from Hungary, USA, Austria, Germany or Spain. According to an international report published in 2013, seven out of ten people in the world report that they have a positive attitude toward entrepreneurship.[133]

Europeans have a more positive attitude to entrepreneurship than Americans, but more Americans than Europeans work in

---

133 The Amway Global Entrepreneurship Report 2013 was commissioned by Amway from the GfK research institute. GfK interviewed in person or by phone 26,009 persons in 24 different countries.

their own companies. These results are particularly contradictory when one looks at the most pro-entrepreneur nation, Denmark. Eighty-nine percent of Danes report that they have a positive attitude toward entrepreneurship. However, when it is time to found a company, Danes are nowhere to be seen. Denmark is in the lowest (4%) band of countries in terms of the number of people founding companies. In other words, Danes have a positive attitude to the idea of founding a company, but prefer to watch from the peanut gallery while someone else files the company papers with the local registry office.[134] Danes are the world's best armchair entrepreneurs.

However, it really might not matter whether you have an positive attitude towards entrepreneurship, since this number has – as the Danes have mercifully proven – no direct connection to the number of people who are or have been entrepreneurs. And even a bigger thing lurking behind these numbers is the discrepancy with the two herds of people: the ones who have thought about founding a company and those who have actually done it. And that might be a big problem.

Whether one dreams about founding a company or actually goes ahead with it is affected by many factors, such as lack of a concept or funding, but one in particular seems to be key: fear of failure.[135] However, there are many different kinds of fear that fit inside the international fear factor (70%). The answers given by respondents were reasonable: money worries, threat of

---

134 This survey did not have a question on how Finns felt about an entrepreneur succeeding. That is quite a different matter.

135 However, the survey forms for example lacked the alternative "too much bother" to the question of why a respondent, despite a positive attitude to entrepreneurship, had not founded a company.

bankruptcy, anxiousness over the effects of the financial crisis, fear of becoming unemployed and fear of ending up in court proceedings. However, there are also deeper, underlying reasons: some were afraid they would end up disappointed and lose self-esteem, while others were afraid they would let others down and lose their families. Many respondents also mentioned fear of losing one's reputation or of not getting another chance.[136] When one thinks about these reasons, it is understandable that people are not keen to found companies.

Americans, who are second to last in attitudes to entrepreneurship, are not afraid of founding a company or of their company failing. Only 37% of Americans reported that fear of failure affected their decision not to found a company. Meanwhile, in Japan the situation is very different. As many as 94% indicated that fear of failure was the biggest reason why they had not founded their own company. European is a lot more fearful than Americans when it comes to starting your own business (73%), and on an international scope the average is 70%. The situation is the following: if you get 100 people together, 70 of them will leave when you start handing out the company founding forms. Nor can they be blamed for that, if one looks at the raw figures.[137] Of all the companies founded today, only one to three will remain in 10 years.

———————

136 Out of a total of 26,009 respondents, the answers were as follows: 41% were afraid of money troubles and the threat of bankruptcy, 31% of the economic crisis, 15% of becoming unemployed and 13% of being sued. Fourteen percent were afraid of becoming disappointed and losing self confidence, 9% were afraid of disappointing others and losing their families, 6% were afraid of losing their reputations and 6% feared they would get no second chance if they failed. Even though the totals seem to be over 100%, some respondents were afraid of more than one thing.

137 It will probably not help that I am showing the fears of would be entrepreneurs to be quite justified.

The 30 potential entrepreneurs remaining do not let the numbers stop them. Still, another 22 decide to give up due to bureaucracy, lack of a concept or some other reason. Now only 8 people remain, looking confused at each other. Right now, it is these eight we must depend on to create the jobs of tomorrow and to build a firm foundation for the economy. Despite their confusion, they sign the company papers.[138] The cost of fear equals everything we lose when those 70 people leave. And their leaving will cost us a great deal.

6.

What would the impact be if a larger number of potential entrepreneurs – i.e., those who might seriously consider founding a company – actually went ahead and did it, rather than just gushing about entrepreneurship in surveys?[139]

---

138 Based on the Amway Entrepreneurial Gap calculation, in which the number of people who have founded companies is subtracted from those with a positive attitude to entrepreneurship.

139 We also toyed around with some numbers. If our numbers game is even partly true, it seems that lowering the threshold to becoming an entrepreneur could prove extremely profitable for everyone. At present, we have an approximately 4,000 net increase in companies in Finland every year. At this rate, we have managed to reach 260,000 companies. When we compare this number to the Finnish gross national product, we can see that the value of one company in the long run is 150,000 per year.
Let us imagine that out of 170,000 people thinking about founding a company, 20,000 would go along with it, rather than the 12,000 we have at present. After ten years, 6,000 of them would remain. Therefore, based on these figures, the effect on the economy would be 19 billion euros, and GDP per capita would grow from the current 35,600 euros to 38,100 euros. Based on Hietala's figures, obstacles, the most important of which is fear, carry an immense financial cost. In addition, fears affect companies and their profitability in other ways in addition to the number of companies being founded. Which is to say, they affect companies from the inside.

One hint might come from the work of Mirjam van Praag, who in 2007 tried to figure out the value of entrepreneurship by conducting a review of high-quality research papers. Praag and co-author Peter Varsloot concluded in their discussion paper [140] that entrepreneurs do indeed bring some value to the table, and a very specific value at that: "they engender relatively much employment creation, productivity growth and produce and commercialize high quality innovations. And there is another very important value that entrepreneurs provide in the economy: entrepreneurial firms produce spillovers that affect regional employment growth rates of all companies in the region in the long run."

The fears of potential entrepreneurs fall into three categories: there are the ones who fear the financial consequences of failure, the ones that fear the psychological implications of failure and the ones who fear the social impact on their family, friends and co-workers.

Some people like Taneli Tikka are able to face the risk and look upon it as a learning experience. But for some it seems to be too much. Risk is always part of doing business, but is the fear of having to bear that risk (especially financial) for the rest of our life or for an unreasonably long time profitable for society any longer? If you take a close look at the work of Mirjam van Praag, there is a reason to believe that we would be better if we would work to reduce fear both on the individual and cultural side.

---

140 Van Praag, C.M. & Versloot, P. (2007), *What is the value of entrepreneurship: A review of recent research Small Business Economics*, 29 (4), pp. 351-382

The relationship with failure seems to be very different in the US compared to Europe or in the extreme case of Japan. One reason for this could be the different cultures of these countries. Researchers noticed that if there was a strong culture of uncertainty avoidance, the fear of failure tended to be high as well. To put it bluntly, you could say that the US operates with a different paradigm than the rest of the world, more or less. The cultural and policy context in the US indicate an evolution-based model: some companies die, while a small number survive. However, those who die have given their own contribution to the evolutionary process. In order for there to be as many entrepreneurs as possible, those who have failed are encouraged to keep on trying, along with those who succeed. According to urban legends, it is hard to get funded in Silicon Valley if you do not have at least one bankruptcy to your name. On the other hand, other countries have more or less a legacy model, with long enduring financial and legal consequences. This is particularly the case in states that punish failed entrepreneurs through bankruptcy legislation.[141]

Professor Dr. Isabell M. Welpe from the Technical university of Munich calls for a culture that values entrepreneurship, encourages potential entrepreneurs and helps them to overcome the fears of an uncertain future.

---

141 In some countries, being a partner in a firm that goes bankrupt may for example affect the price at which banks give financing and how easy it is to get it. A bankruptcy may stay on your credit record for up to five years.

Intelligent People in Stupid Groups

1.

Groups tend to be fairly stupid. This is almost the only conclusion one can draw after having spent a year or more in working life. Although, to be fair, groups are also often fairly intelligent. This is almost the only conclusion one can draw after having spent a year or more in working life. Moreover, this is a difficult problem to address, as no one seems to know what makes a group intelligent or stupid.

A group acting stupidly is often harangued for not having enough talented people. People also often refer to some kind of magical glue called "chemistry." Smart people and chemistry – those are the makings of group intelligence. The first is a matter of selection, and the second is some sort of magic.

On the other hand, what if we have been looking at group intelligence from the wrong point of view? What if group intelligence is something we can actually affect to a much greater degree than we might think?

Psychologists have long thought that individual mental capacity is a combination of different abilities. But there is a factor that is central to our intelligence, and that is the g-factor, i.e., general intelligence. In short, if your g-factor is high, you are good at a diverse range of cognitive tasks. G-factor is well measured in IQ tests, but no one had studied the question whether there is a similar deciding factor with regards to group intelligence – at least not until Anita Williams Woolley from the Universities of Boston and Pittsburgh organised a series of tests to investigate just that question.

Woolley set out to find whether there is a set of corresponding factors for general intelligence in group settings, and if so, what factors predictably determined a group's intelligence. It would of course be easy to assume that group intelligence could be increased by bringing in a super smart people, or by raising the average IQ of the group. However, what Woolley found was that neither of these was the best approach.

Woolley gathered 152 similar groups of two to five people to carry out assigned tasks as well as possible. The assignments have been chosen from among tasks intended to measure the various aspects of intelligence.[142] The tasks assigned to the group varied from creative thinking and spatial awareness to complex group coordination tasks. As a final task, the group was asked to play a round of checkers.[143] The tasks were scored in such a way that you get the most points for the smartest and most creative solutions.

---

142 McGrath Task Circumplex.

143 The test starts with a classic tile test, where the group has to think of as many uses for a tile as possible. Next there is a simple intelligence test, where the group is asked to come up with one right answer for each question. This is a conventional intelligence test, but as it is done in a group there is some additional pressure. The third test measures moral decision making. The group is presented with a situation where a University basketball player has bribed a teacher in order to get a better grade. The situation is to be assessed according to five different themes, with five options for each. The group is given scores for how well they are able to combine the interests of the different parties and to find a fair and just punishment. The next test is familiar to anyone who has worked on shared documents on Google Drive – they are tasked with reproducing the complex text given to them. Then they are tasked with planning an optimally efficient shopping trip, and finally they play a game of checkers.

Woolley conducted dozens of tests with 699 people. They confirmed her hypothesis that there is more behind group ability than the raw computing power of the individual brains in the group. The results were unequivocal: the highest IQ in the group did not determine group intelligence, nor did having a group where all members had above-average intelligence.[144] The common denominator for group intelligence was found elsewhere, and Woolley considers these findings to be the best predictive factors for a group's intellectual capacity.

Some test participants did the NEO test, which measures social sensitivity among other things. The results of this test turned out to be decisive. Social sensitivity had a significant effect on the results of a given group. However, Woolley dug in deeper in order to discover what smart groups were doing differently than the others. Test participants were asked to wear a recorder that taped everything that the test subject said while the group was working on its tasks. The researchers were particularly interested in how the group divided speaking turns among themselves. Was one group member dominating the discussion, or was everyone allowed to get a word in? After the tests, the computer program analysed the material. When the statistical analysis was finished, Woolley and her group were able to pick three previous points from the masses of data.

According to Woolley, group intelligence is primarily affected by three factors. The first of these is conversational turn taking, i.e., how speaking turns are divided. The more evenly turns are divided, the more intelligently the group operates. If one or two

---

144 The intelligence of individual group members matters, though not as much as one might think.

socially dominant people speak more than the others, then the group regresses to stupidity.

The social sensitivity of group members was another factor. If the average social sensitivity of the group is high, then the group functions better. Social sensitivity means for example that group members are aware of each others' feelings and are able, for example, to lighten the mood with a joke when necessary or to steer the discussion in a more constructive direction without steamrolling over other people.

A third factor uncovered by Woolley's analysis was the number of women in a group. However, this observation correlated so strongly with the social sensitivity of group members that it belongs more properly with that factor. Woolley explains the connection between these two factors by the fact that women are more socially sensitive.[145]

There are many layers to these test results. It is clear that a group acts more intelligently when the ideas and thoughts brought by group members to their shared task are evenly divided and no one dominates socially.

One way to approach this is by thinking of creativity as the ability to combine things in a new way. After all, this is often what happens when a team works together. Each group member's brain contains a number of concepts, anecdotes, ways of thinking, schema, practical experiences, hunches, memes and facts. The way groups often work is that the most socially strong individual dominates the discussion. However, when only one

---

145 Of course, at this point one might ask whether women are genetically programmed to be more socially sensitive, or whether our culture conditions us in such a way that these qualities are considered more acceptable and preferable for women.

person is speaking, the group often ends up with a one-sided, narrow view that is therefore often flawed. However, if group members are able to evenly contribute, the end result is a more balanced, pluralistic perspective, and the number of new combinations increases. If a group has six duplo bricks, the kind of structure they can make out of them is very different than if they had a 1,200-piece Lego Architecture Studio set.

However, all of this is not enough. In addition, the group must be able to work together in such a way that they combine the pieces in a sensible manner. Not all solutions are worth trying, and the closer one is to a final result, the more critical the conversation tends to be. As the team gets closer to h-hour, ideas are worked on and killed. If the group has been working on an idea together, then a sense of trust will have formed between group members. On the basis of this trust, the group can engage in extremely critical discussions without any group member feeling like he or she is being personally attacked. This is precisely the factor that many creative and socially dominant people miss.[146] It is not a question of adopting a soft, "anything goes" mindset, but about trust between group members so that the end result is a team where people can argue about ideas without breaching the mutual trust inside the group. In a smart group, a person's identity is not bolstered or threatened by the ideas he or she expresses.

---

146 Yes and no. Steve Jobs was socially dominant. One can achieve results in many different ways; however, the question remains at what price and whether anyone wants to work at a place where there is only one brain and the rest are merely hands. There are few creative geniuses, but there are groups everywhere, and any group can function more intelligently by using better models of cooperation.

2.

The most important lesson we can draw from Woolley's study is her prime commandment, which if followed will improve group intelligence: distribute speaking turns in conversation more evenly. Nevertheless, if we want to find an answer to why social sensitivity is so important for a group's ability, we need to look elsewhere.

"I am interested in what people would do if they weren't afraid," says Stephen Porges, whose ideas we touched upon earlier. His polyvagal theory has, over many years of research, come to the point where he is able to say with certainty that our nervous system is responsible for the nature of our social relationships. Our nervous system evaluates, selects and directs our interactions with other people. Every situation we are in is classified as safe, dangerous or lethally dangerous.

Even though the evolution of human beings is a narrative of dangers, the mammalian nervous system did not, according to Porges, develop solely to protect us from danger. More recently developed nervous structures have a social task: interaction and forming bonds. The new layers did not replace the old – the nerve branches we inherited from reptiles, and the survival mechanisms connected with them, still remain.[147] In this new stage of our development, our nervous system had to develop so that it could regulate our body in such a way that quick shifts in our autonomous state were possible. It takes us a split second to move from relaxed social interaction to full combat readiness.

------

147 Porges, S., *The Polyvagal Theory: Neurophysiological Foundations of Emotions, Attachment, Communication, and Self-regulation,* 2011.

Our nervous system, among other things, determines how intelligently we behave in social situations and how intelligently the group we belong to operates. It is our nervous system that decides which of the three available strategies we pick in a given situation. If our nervous system flags the situation as safe, it sets our body in a state of social interaction. According to Porges, a person's nervous system is only in this state when a situation has been interpreted as safe. We need to be in this state to have anything like what Woolley describes as social sensitivity. However, if the situation seems even a little dangerous, we regress to defensive models. Even slight danger signals (for example an expressionless face, a nasty memory of a similar situation, the body language of a companion, etc.) can make the members of a group retract into their shells, freeze up or engage in a social counter-attack. The central nervous system is tasked with preparing the body for mobilisation or paralysis. These are not skills that one learns, but rather part of our genetic legacy. They are also completely automatic. It is easy to observe these defence models by watching animals. However, it is harder to spot them with human beings, because we as intensely social animals have learned to hide our true emotions by reducing non-verbal communication or by putting on a smile even when we are boiling inside. We are even able to control our reactions with our thoughts. In any case, our nervous system does not miss these cues, and they have an immediate effect on our behaviour.

3.

"If you can't open your mouth during a meeting, then you may be in the wrong job." This sentence is, in a nutshell, how I used to think as a young manager. I believed that work is a struggle between ideas and people, where the strongest (ideas and people) win. However, over the years the evidence has piled up against this notion. Small, almost imperceptible changes transformed editorial meetings from war to cooperation. This had a particularly large effect on those members of the team who had contributed very little when work had been a battleground. When everyone's ideas were discussed evenly and social shenanigans like shooting down other people's ideas were weeded out, people became less afraid that their ideas would be thought dumb or insignificant. As people became less afraid, they started to take more risks, which produced more vigorous conversations and better ideas. However, the most essential thing was that, despite being in a risky situation, people felt psychologically safe.

According to Porges, high level creativity is only possible when a person feels secure. We may be capable of manufacturing goods and developing our potential while our defensive reactions are active, but it is only the feeling of security that gives a solid foundation on which one can build something original.

It may be difficult to accept Porges' view if one has never worked in a group that manages to stay at the level of social interaction even in a threatening situation. In other words, group members manage to keep things safe even when the situation is dangerous.

Let us take performing in front of the TV cameras, for example. Only a complete lunatic would feel safe on TV. It is a high risk media, where a single mistake can lose you your reputation and lead to an eternal stigma. I know this, as among other things I host the comedy panel tv-show called The Good and the Bad News. The show is based on improvisation relating to fresh news and science topics. It requires that every single one of our panelists and I as a host are incisive, dares to blurt out the idea they just had, and trusts that nothing catastrophic will follow. This would just not work in a hostile environment. On the other hand, the show would be boring if everyone agreed with each other. However, when all members of the group feel (sufficiently) safe with each other, they can say whatever they like to each other without endangering their relationship. All of this is underpinned by trust in the mutual respect between team members, and in the fact that everyone has the same goal, i.e., turning out a good program, rather than in upsetting the social order. This also applies to writing the script, which often involves heated arguments and even shouted discussions. One can appreciate candid talk when one feels that the situation is safe and stays at the level of social interaction.

It may be difficult to understand how even tiny danger signals affect the level at which we can use our individual capacity and what the group is capable of together.

One thing that we constantly assess[148] in a group situation is our own imaginary status in the group. If we feel that our position is getting weaker, it may reduce the amount of capacity we are able to use. For this to happen, it takes even less than disapproving looks or belittling comments.

I have been fascinated by this observation for decades. It forces you to think about the two sides of fear in work communities. Perhaps the fear one sees in work communities is not just or primarily the problem of those who are afraid, but first and foremost

---

148 Consciously or subconsciously.

the problem of the ones who are responsible for evoking the fear in others. In a work community, fear is everybody's problem.

Where fear has been used in a manner bordering on mental abuse, normalization begins with establishing a principle of perfect openness and increasing transparency. In addition to non-violent communication, you can help people in a work community set their defence systems to a state that allows for higher intellectual functions by creating a safe space and increasing mutual trust, removing the stakes from social situation, concentrating on the things you can affect and emphasising dialogue, rather than constant debate. It is crucial to remember that the opposite of a frightening situation is not a critique-free, soft, lukewarm hippie co-existence, but rather a state where people feel safe even when they are in a socially threatening situation.

4.

I have gone on record as stating that meetings are poison for the intellect, draining a person's intelligence and soul. It is easy to blame bad leadership, a sloppy agenda, or ever-present wireless networks for the bad quality of co-operation. I certainly cannot deny that these have an effect on the quality of business meetings, but the problem solving ability of participants may plummet for other reasons as well, such as how worried a participant is about his or her social status in the group.

Increasingly, creative, knowledge, and brain work are not done alone. People spend from an estimated four hours a week (regular office worker) to up to four days per week (expert)[149] in meetings. In academia, the size of research groups has grown 20% per year, and in many professions where people used to work alone, such as coders, they are now working in groups. Furthermore, decisions are not made in a vacuum either. The Swedish may be notorious for their marathon consensus building, but others are also increasingly attempting to form a shared view and decision together. It is therefore far from irrelevant how much of our intellect we are able to use while working with others.

A test conducted at the Carilion Research Institute at Virginia Tech seems to indicate that even the slightest doubt that one might be dumber than other group members, and therefore socially below them, can make group members dumb.[150] A team led by Kenneth Kishida selected students for the test with an average IQ of 126. During the test, every group member did intelligence tests to their best ability. After each individual test, a statistic would pop up on the screen of the test computer, showing their ranking within their own five member reference group. The researchers were not cruel enough to show participants names, but they were cruel enough to clearly indicate the participant's own ranking. Kishida was particularly interested in whether knowledge about one's own intelligence in com-

---

149 For example Romano Jr, N.C., Nunamaker Jr, J.F., "Meeting Analysis: Findings from Research and Practice," proceedings of the 34th Hawaii International Conference on System Sciences 2001 http://www.basexblog.com/2010/11/04/our-findings/

150 Kishida, K.T., Yang, D., Hunter Quartz, K., Quartz, S.R., Montague, P. R., "Implicit signals in small group settings and their impact on the expression of cognitive capacity and associated brain responses," Phil. Trans. R. Soc. B (2012) 367, 704–716.

parison with other group members would affect how well a person continued to do in the test. It turns out that it did – to a shocking degree.

Based on the results, test participants were finally divided into two groups: those who did well at the tests and those who did poorly. However, even the highest scoring participants were not immune to evaluation. During the test, their IQ decreased by an average of eight points.[151] Social pressure seemed to affect their performance to some degree. When it comes to the other group, a word like "affect" would be misplaced – their performance collapsed. IQ came down by an average of 17.4 points.

In our society, it is important to be intelligent. Intelligence is highly rated in education, job interviews and public discussions. However, even if an IQ test is a valid metric, it only measures intelligence in an isolated test at that precise moment. It does not tell the whole truth about how much of a person's intellectual potential is available in a given real life situation.[152]

According to Kishida, their test draws attention to the unexpected and dramatic effect of even slight cues pointing to social status on a person's ability. The test also shows the mechanism that turns reasonably smart people into fairly slow thinkers. According to the researchers, social cues seemed to affect many areas of the brain, but particularly the amygdala, the orbitofrontal cortex and the nucleus accumbensis. In other words, those parts of the brain that we know are related to pleasure, problem solving and processing emotions. The orbitofrontal cortex has a

---

151 +- 4 points.

152 This may also be the reason why a high IQ does not always correlate with success.

particularly big role in problem solving.[153] It has, among other things, a huge effect on working memory, which is considered a key component of intelligence.[154] The better a person's working memory, the more intelligent they are.

During the test, pressure relating to social status increased activity in the amygdala, with a corresponding decrease in the area of the orbitofrontal cortex. When it comes to problem solving, this is pretty much the worst possible combination.

In addition to this finding, perhaps the most interesting part of the test was that, when it came to those test participants with the best results in the test, there was a change in the activity levels of their amygdala and in their test scores. This change became increasingly pronounced as the test continued. For this group, their amygdalas were at full alert at the beginning of the test, and they were scoring slightly less than others. Things changed about halfway through the test. For those who ultimately scored the best, there was a slight decrease in amygdala activity, and an increase in activity in the thinking parts of the brain. Meanwhile, the other group had high amygdala activity throughout the test, with performance that got worse toward the end of the test. The

---

153 For example Ashby, F.G., Ell, S.W., Valentin, V.V., Casale, M.B., "FROST: A Distributed Neurocomputational Model of working memory maintenance," *Journal of Cognitive Neuroscience,* Volume 17 Issue 11, November 2005, 1728–1743.

154 The connection between working memory or short-term memory, processing speed and intelligence has been studied for example by Kyllonen, P.C., Christal, R.E., "Reasoning ability is little more than working-memory capacity," *Intelligence* Volume 14, Issue 4, October–December 1990, 389–433, as well as Fry, A.F., Hale, S., "Processing Speed, Working Memory, and Fluid Intelligence: Evidence for a Developmental Cascade," *Psychological Science,* 01/1996; 7(4), 237–241 jand Conway, A.R.A., *Biol Psychol.* 2000 Oct; 54(1–3): 1–34., Cowan, N., Buntinga, M.F., Therriault, D.J., Minkoff S.R.B., "A latent variable analysis of working memory capacity, short-term memory capacity, processing speed, and general fluid intelligence," *Intelligence* 30 (2002) 163–183.

main difference between the two groups was that those who got better as the test continued had an active nucleus accumbens. We do not precisely know what this observation means, but we do know that activity in this area is connected with rewards and pleasure.

Even though the test situation was artificial and there was only a small number of participants, the test reveals the warning cues to factors potentially leading to crippled cognitive capacity. Kishida's tests also seem to correlate with many of the other studies and anecdotes presented in this book: performance in various tests measuring problem solving ability weakens when fear, anxiety and stress increase over a given level, where the additional energy provided by them no longer sharpens one's senses or attention to detail. Group pressure is a significant stressor. Concealing one's weaknesses and ignorance may sometimes be a sensible strategy, but it does not increase group intelligence. Intelligent groups may have something in common: the defence systems of group members stay switched off, and the higher functions of their brains[155] remain powered up. Those who do not manage this must pay a great cost due to decreased cognitive capacity.

---

155 For example, the prefrontal cortex referred to above.

I Can Smell Your Fear

1.

Not only does fear control our actions, but it can also control the actions of others. Similarly, someone else's fear may affect how we behave even before we are actually consciously aware of the fear. Knowing that there is a threat nearby has been vital for our survival, so vital that the message had to travel from one member of the herd to another. Our bodies made sure that even a blocked communication channel or two would not interfere. When we experience fear and our various survival mechanisms start activating, fear can be seen, heard and smelled – quite literally.

If a member of our herd is afraid, it serves as a signal that there are threats around us. This way, the systems overseeing dangerous and deadly situations can get a head start. They arrange resources (oxygen, energy, blood flow, cognitive processes, senses) before we actually consciously notice anything. Those who stopped to think in dangerous situation have mostly been weeded out by evolution, while those with sensitive defence mechanisms were able to pass on their genes to the next generations.

We have very effective systems for detecting the fear of others. When it comes to fear, all of our sensory channels are highly receptive, even though it would be sufficient to receive the message through one channel for our body to raise its alert level.[156] Most

---

156 de Groot J.H.B., Semin G.R., Smeets M.A.M. (2013 July 15) "I can see, hear, and smell your fear: comparing olfactory and audiovisual media in fear communication," *Journal of Experimental Psychology*: General, Vol 143(2), Apr 2014, 825–834.

of these mechanisms are fully automated, and some of them seem almost as outlandish as jedi senses.

Observing the expressions and gestures of others is an important survival strategy, as they reveal, among many other things, fear.[157] When fear takes control, the muscles of a person's face engage in a feat of amazing cooperation. The human face has 46 muscle units. While you can express for example joy by using two muscle units, fear activates six. Paul Ekman, who has studied how the face expresses emotion, has found that fear takes control of muscle units 1, 2, 4, 5, 20 and 26.[158] These muscle movements are visible as a wrinkling of the brow, as well as the eyebrows rising straight up and drawing close together. In addition, the eyelids rise, showing the whites of the eyes above the irises. Not much happens to the cheeks, but the mouth opens and the muscles controlling the lips pull the lips wide.[159]

As a person grows up, they learn to hide conscious signals of their emotions, but body language is harder to change. Through their work on expressions and emotions, Silvan Tomkins and Paul Ekman learned a great deal about micro-expressions. Micro-expressions are split second glimmers on a person's face. They are those minute cues that the main character in the *Mentalist* knows how to read. He looks for hidden signals in the muscles

---

157 Gestures and expressions convey important information concerning another person's internal state. For example, are they hiding aggression or speaking the truth?

158 The muscles in Latin: *frontalis pars medialis, frontalis pars lateralis, depressor glaballea, depressor supercilii, corregator supercilii, levator palpebrae superioris, tarsalis superior, risorius and platysma.*

159 One can see from Paul Ekman's pictures that expressions could often be interpreted based on much less infor-mation, such as merely the eyebrows or the eyes, but for some reason expressions are conveyed in such a way that nothing is left unclear.

of a person's face, as well as in their pupils and body language. For example, if your mouth is smiling but your *musculus orbicularis oculi* contracts, it means the smile is not real, but you are instead trying to conceal something. It is a fictitious TV show, but the principle holds true. It is also true that some people have either naturally or through practice acquired the ability to read micro-expressions on an amazing level. However, most of us register this contradiction between expressions and words through a feeling of wrongness. It is almost as if one were trying to screw a bolt in, out of groove, using a long ratchet. The bolt turns, sinking into the hole drilled for it, but something is not quite right.

The systems that regulate the facial muscles also regulate the larynx and the vocal chords. The parasympathetic nerve system that regulates our vital functions connects the heart, through the vagal nerve, with the vocal chords. In other words, the same nerve that controls how fast our heart beats also has an effect on how our larynx and vocal chords work. Consequently, your voice may quiver or break when you are afraid. Similarly, the middle ear, which receives human voices, is connected to the vagal nerve. In other words, our nervous system communicates with itself through the language of fear.

What this means is that our gestures, the timing of our movements, our positions, our words and tones of voice reveal our inner world to those around us who, if they are sensitive enough, can read these cues or be unknowingly affected by them.

The only thing missing is the ability to smell fear. However, if you ask researchers Wen Zhou and Denise Chen, they can tell you that we can in fact do this – we just do not know about it.

2.

Pheromones are chemicals that insects and many animals use to communicate with each other. For example, dogs have something called a Jacobson's organ that detects and interprets smell-based messages. Animals can use pheromones for example to locate food after one member of their group has found it. Pheromones are used to mark territory, to attract a mate, and – when danger strikes – as something of an air raid siren.

Many dog or horse owners will tell you that animals can smell your fear. This is not entirely true. While animals can smell fear, they can only smell it on members of their own species.[160] A dog or horse can sense a person's fear, but it seems that this is because a dog recognises certain expressions and sudden movements, while a horse easily reacts to having a rider on its back who is moving around nervously. The debate about whether animals can smell a person's fear goes on, but I am considerably more interested in whether fear can spread through scents from one person to another.

There is no proper scientific evidence when it comes to humans and pheromones. The problem is physiological: human beings do not have a functioning Jacobson's organ, which is needed to identify pheromones.[161] While some people do possess this organ, no nerves connect it to the brains. It just sits there in one's palate like an evolutionary relic. This has led to a debate on whether we are able to communicate through smells.

---

160 For example, according to Nancy Diehl, a researcher at Penn State University.

161 When a snake flicks its tongue, it does not do so in order to send shivers of fear down our spines. Nor is a snake's tongue forked because of its evil nature. A snake flicks its tongue in order to sniff out prey and to find its way. Scents direct it to food

In any case, according to scholars we can be fairly certain in any case that signals spread through scents are not as dominant with human beings as with other animals. However, that does not mean that they are meaningless. The solution to this debate can be found somewhere between the two extremes. Humans communicate through smells, but the signals we emit into the air are much weaker and less effective than animal pheromones, so pheromone researcher Sarah Woodley prefers to speak of them as chemosignals.[162]

Even though scents have less effect with us than with other animals, their effect on us is neither non-existent nor insignificant. Wen Zhou and Denise Chen have carried out a series of scent experiments, where they exposed women to male sweat that had been collected when the men had either been happy or terrified. [163] The women participating in the test were asked to recognise the happy and frightened expressions in various images while they were exposed to these different sweat samples. Interestingly enough, the sweat or its origins did not seem to

---

and shelter. Its tongue is forked for the same reason that we have two eyes and two ears: with two points of observation, one can more easily and precisely determine direction and distance than with only one point. The snake thrusts its tongue into the Jacobson's organ in the roof of its mouth. Thanks to its forked tongue, the snake can easily "see" from which direction a scent is coming from.

162 This word is from Sarah Woodley's article in the *Tiede* magazine from 2009. Chemosignals can transmit information, and their use can be detected in brain images even when the person does not know what he or she is smelling. However, they do not determine human behaviour in the same way as that of some animals. For example, we cannot find our way to the grocery store using chemosignals. Recommendations from friends, street signs and advertisements generally work better.

163 Different researchers have come up with ever more outlandish ways of collecting fear chemosignals and proving their effects. Wen Zhou and Denise Chen, referred to above, put highly absorbent artificial silk and polyester mix pads in men's armpits and showed them a bloodcurdling horror film. They were then

have an effect when the expressions and body language of the people in the images were clear. On the other hand, when it came to ambiguous expressions, the test participants seemed to more easily interpret them as fear. According to Zhou and Chen, this proves that smell directs our social interpretations when our other senses are weak.[164]

However, the key question is how all of this affects human behaviour. Based on Zhou's and Chen's test, we can assume that in a group situation, the bodily alert level of other people present will rise if someone in the group is sending fear signals.[165] The question is, do the fear signals of other improve our performance or ruin it? We have already seen what can happen to a group's intelligence or to an individual person if group ties are not strong or if a person is afraid of being evaluated by others.

In one of her earlier studies, Denise Chen investigated the effects of the smell of fear on a person's cognitive capacity. Her results were ambiguous. Women's performance increased with

---

given new pads and shown some slapstick comedy, which naturally made them happy – possible chemosignals relating to happiness were collected from the pads. Pads with fear sweat and joy sweat were then brought to be sniffed by the women participating in the experiment.

164 However, is this a chemosignal almost as powerful as pheromones or is the criticism levelled against the study by other researchers correct: what if it is a case of the amount and not the quality of the sweat? The pulses of the men did not rise, and they did not sweat in the same way when watching the comedy film, whereas they had elevated pulse and increased sweating while afraid, which are natural ways for the fear glands to behave in response to a fear reaction. According to this criticism, test subjects ought to react in the same way to the sweat of athletes and people who have been afraid – however, this is not the case. Many tests investigating the existence and effects of fear chemosignals have used the sweat of athletes. Despite the bad reputation of locker room stink, test subjects did not react at all in the same way as they did to fear sweat, leading to different expressions, changes in behaviour, and activation of certain areas of the brain.

165 Particularly where other signals relating to feelings are vague or scarce. Which is the case in interactions between people at the average Finnish workplace.

a word recognition task after they had been exposed to fear sweat. They were more precise and as fast as with neutral sweat. However, this was only the case with clear tasks. The moment the words became more emotionally ambiguous and similar to everyday challenges, they started to get slower.[166] According to the researchers, this is because when danger threatens, people adopt strategies that prepare them to meet the threat – their attention to detail increases, and they start acting more carefully.

It is important to distinguish between a fear chemosignal and the actual fear reaction. In some studies where researchers used brain imaging equipment, they noticed that "smelling fear" activated the same areas of the brain used for processing fear signals. On the other hand, these parts of the brain do more than just handle fear signals. Indeed, Chen's study seems to prove the same fact we have encountered time and again: controllable fear increases a person's activation level. It gives you energy and can improve your performance. It gets the engine started like a few cups of coffee on an empty stomach in the morning, even if one may wind up feeling rather ill. On the other hand, when it comes to harder tasks and the fear factor increases, fear has the opposite effect.

This negative effect can be seen for example in how a person starts to take increasingly large risks. In a study directed by Katrin Haegler at the University of Munich, fear chemosignals caused exactly this effect. In a double-blind test organised by Haegler,[167] participants were asked to take part in a gambling

---

166 Chen, D., Katdare, A., Lucas, N., "Chemosignals of Fear Enhance Cognitive Performance in Humans," *Chem Senses*, 2006 Jun; 31(5): 415–423.

167 Haegler, K., Zernecke, R., Kleemann, A.M., Albrecht, J., Pollatos, O., Brückmann, H., Wiesmann, M., "No fear no risk! Human risk behavior is affected by chemosensory anxiety signals," *Neuropsychologia*, 2010 Nov; 48(13): 3901–3908.

simulation.[168] Haegler knew in advance that those who had higher trait anxiety would tend to take larger risks.[169] Moreover, she wanted to see whether the stakes set by healthy individuals would change if they were unknowingly exposed to the smell based chemosignals of another person's fear. The test bore out this hypothesis. The group set higher stakes when fear was in the air compared to the occasions when they were breathing workout sweat or neutral air. Haegler and her team noticed that fear and anxiety, fear-related chemosignals and decision making activated the same sub-areas of the brain.[170]

Based on these and many other studies on chemosignals, we can conclude that human beings really do send chemical fear signals, which other people can receive either consciously or unconsciously.

The cost of fear is that fear-related signals have a negative effect on decision making. The smell of fear activates the amygdala, which starts to send danger-related signals. As a result, some people became timid, while others take rash risks, and everyone slows down. Indeed, the fact that we slow down seems to be more

---

168 Haegler's Risk Game.

169 British psychologist Kevin Dutton is one of the researchers who have carried out tests with fear sweat. Dutton made a comparison of the effects of sweat from people who had watched the *Candyman* movie to sweat from people who had been running on the treadmill. This comparison is interesting, as he wanted to see how sub-conscious signals affect how people behave while doing the Cambridge Gamble Task, i.e., a computer-controlled game testing decision-making ability under pressure. Those subjected to fear sweat played more carefully than those subjected to treadmill sweat. Psychopaths did not react to fear sweat in any way whatsoever. I contacted Dutton to ask him about the tests mentioned in his book, the *Wisdom of Psychopaths*. He stated that his results were only preliminary, and that research was ongoing

170 On this point, her results deviated from the preliminary findings of Dutton's work with psychopaths. However, they did have something in common: in both studies, it took longer to make decisions when the smell of fear was in the air.

important than the effects on decision making.[171] In the tests, the differences in durations are very small, but still seem to indicate that the brain uses more energy to make a decision. Working with emotions is exhausting, and the areas used for controlling emotions get tired.[172]

Even though fear-related smells do not overwhelm us, fear-related recognition and defence mechanisms are so strong and so powerful that they affect our behaviour. These signals penetrate our nervous systems either in such a way that we bypass the messages carried to us by smells and we process the information calmly and analytically, or, when we receive an alarming message, we launch the necessary defence mechanisms.

Everything we have gone over so far seems to indicate that life would be easier if we were not afraid. Fortunately, this is not the case. Based on the evidence, fearlessness is not something that anyone should aspire to.

3.

A fear study patient called "SM," an under-fifty-year-old woman, is one of the few people considered by scientists to be truly fearless. SM is completely normal when it comes to her

---

171 The results on the effects are often contradictory

172 The prefrontal cortex controls the emotions. For example, if we need to conquer our fears or handle negative emotions, this area becomes active. Most studies have found that if this area is "overexercised," it seems to grow tired and the person starts to act more impulsively. For example, Baumeister has written on the subject: *Willpower. Rediscovering the greatest human strength*, 2011.

intelligence, memory, language and observational skills, but she is not afraid of anything, and does not learn through fear. She is incapable of recognising fear on another person's face and acts abnormally in situations where people's behaviour is guided by fear. SM has been diagnosed with the extremely rare Urbach-Wiethe disease, which attacks the amygdala and gradually destroys it. Even though research is still on-going on the specific purpose of the amygdala, researchers agree that it seems to have a key role in producing fear-related associations. "Fear-related associations are in the amygdala," according to fear researcher Daniela Schiller. In practice, the amygdala handles fear-based learning, alertness and memory regulation relating to fear stimuli, recognising sources of fear and initiating fear-related behaviours.

However, in effect SM has no amygdala, and a group of researchers are convinced[173] that this is the reason for her abnormal behaviour. There is no lack of evidence for this claim. SM has been tested using a variety of methods over the years, and her case history is a story of fearlessness.

In one memorable field test SM was taken to a store for exotic animals.[174] Even though she had often said that she hates and fears snakes, she eagerly approached the reptiles. When the store owner asked her whether she wanted to hold a snake, she imme-

---

173 There are also scholars, such as Elizabeth Phelps, who are not equally convinced that SM's fearlessness is due to this reason. In her critical writings, Phelps points to her own studies on people suffering from the same disease. Even though subjects had difficult recognising fearful expressions, they were not without fear.

174 Feinstein, J.S., Adolphs, R., Damasio, A.R., Tranel, D., "The human amygdala and the induction and experience of fear," *Curr Biol.*, 2011 Jan 11; 21(1): 34–38.

diately said yes. SM raised a yellow, over a metre long snake in her arms and held it for over three minutes. She stroked its scales and touched its tongue with her hand.[175] "This is so cool!" she said. SM inspected the snake, and with the wriggling animal still in her arms, asked the store owner about the snake's sense of sight and other matters that would have been entirely meaningless for a person paralysed by fear. She seemed almost obsessed with touching and poking the snakes in the store. SM asked a total of 15 times whether she could touch the more dangerous snakes even though the store owner repeatedly told her that some of the larger snakes were dangerous and could bite. She also tried to touch a big tarantula lurking at the bottom of its terrarium, but the store owner managed to stop her. [176]

The researchers noticed that SM did not at any stage show any signs of trying to avoid dangerous animals (or anything else). Quite to the contrary – she seemed to be very keen on getting to know every kind of wriggling or furred, poisonous animal she could find, quite unlike the vast majority of her fellow human

---

175 Even though no images of SM have been released into the public, there are a few photos in the article on her, showing her hands and shirt. She seems quite elegant from her nails, which have been painted with glossy nail varnish. She has had a French manicure, and wears a white shirt. This combination does not give the impression of a wild person or one prone to getting into violent situations. Of course, this might be a conclusion too far simply based on one photo of her hands and nails, but it is nevertheless something that should be taken into account when considering her history. These clues, as well as her lack of a criminal record give the impression that she does not consciously flirt with danger or the dark side of life.

176 A tarantula has never been known to cause a (documented) death, but people are still afraid of spiders, particularly big hairy spiders. Snakes and spiders are the groups of animals that people are most often afraid of, even when there are none in their living environment.

beings. When asked how frightened she felt she was on a scale of 2-10, SM picked the lowest value, 2. [177]

SM made it out of the exotic animal store unharmed. The same cannot be said for all of her moments of fearlessness. As confirmed by police reports, a large woman thoroughly beat her, and she was almost killed in an incident of domestic violence.[178] She has been threatened with a gun and with a knife.

One of the violent incidents she has been involved in took place in a park after nightfall. A man who was sitting on a park bench motioned for her to come closer. When she did, he drew out a knife, pressed it against her throat and threatened to kill her. SM did not react to this attack in any way. When her confused attacker relaxed his grip, she walked calmly away. The next evening, SM walked through the same park. This threatening situation seems to have had as little meaning for her as any other everyday occurrence, for example if one of the laces on her left shoe had happened to come open while she was walking through the park.

SM learns nothing from dangerous situations, even near death incidents. Researchers suspect that decay of the amygdala leaves a person without the evolutionary advantage provided by that part of the brain. SM might in theory live longer as she is less

---

177 SM's family were not surprised by these reactions (or lack thereof). In one article, her son recalled how the children had seen a huge snake on the road. They ran home to tell their mother, who walked up to the snake, picked it up from the tarmac, and then carried it to a nearby patch of grass and set it free. Even though the situation was dangerous, nothing bad happened.

178 Nothing seems to indicate that this mother of two was behaving aggressively.

prone to stress, but she may well die before her time due to the risks that she takes with so little concern.[179]

Fear also seems to some degree to affect the kind of contact we have with other people. In social situations, people usually try to get others to relax and to bring down their defence mechanisms. For this reason, it is important to be able to read other people's fear-related signals and to learn how to act in accordance with them.

When I asked Daniela Schiller about SM,[180] she said that she was surprised about how close to other people SM stands. In fact, she stands well inside the "bubble" that people generally consider to be the comfortable zone where they feel physically safe.[181] SM invades other people's physical space completely without realising it, as due to her decayed amygdala, she is unable to interpret the fear- or aggression-related expressions and gestures of other people.[182] SM does not pull back even though the other person is uncomfortable.

---

179 Researchers have tried to scare SM in many different ways. Once they took her to The Waverly Hills Sanatorium, an old hospital considered one of the most "haunted" houses in the world. SM did not even flinch when the actors hiding in the house jumped at her from behind doors or corners. She walked without any qualms into dark halls, urging the others in the group to follow her. While other group members flinched or screamed due to the actors and special effects in the house, SM actually managed to scare one of the actors. It should therefore come as no surprise that when she was shown some of the scariest scenes from horror movies, she estimated her reaction to them to be 1 on a scale of 1 to 8.

180 Schiller has not personally met SM, but as Schiller has studied the amygdala and its effects on human behaviour, she is quite familiar with this well publicised case.

181 SM stands, on average, 34 cm away from other people, while the normal distance between people in her culture is 64 cm

182 For example recognising alarming micro-expressions on other people's faces.

At last, after numerous failed attempts, researchers manage to actually scare SM. To be more precise, they went further than that, sending SM into a panic.[183] They managed this by changing the consistency of the air she was breathing. SM and a group of other test participants took part in an experiment where they breathed 35% carbon dioxide. It only took eight seconds to send SM into full panic. Through this test, researchers claim they have proved that we have at least two different systems for triggering defensive reactions. One is external, i.e., the one that SM is missing, while the other is internal, picking up lethal danger in other kinds of signals, for example if the the air you are breathing has too much carbon dioxide to support life.[184]

SM's personal history, jumping from one threat to another, and her way of pushing herself into other people's social space are warning examples of what happens if you lack fear or the neurological structures relating to fear. Fear shields us from direct danger, helps us to avoid dangerous situations, and at least the amygdala seems to have some role in assessing social signals. However, this does not stop us from wondering about what life would be like without fear. Each one of us can list situations where we have been bothered by fear or worries. This could be a penalty shot taken under intense pressure in a game of football,

---

183 This was the first time SM experienced fear since her childhood years.

184 However, this came as no surprise to Porges. He also stated that there was no need to take such drastic measures. This method is apparently impossible to resist, because it drives the body into immediate crisis survival state. This also seems to explain why waterboarding is so effective. Waterboarding is a form of torture where the subject is tied down with their head at a downward angle. The subject's head (particularly the nose and mouth) is then covered with a cloth, which is soaked with water. The subject is, in a way, drowning on dry land.

hasty, uncertain answers in a job interview, a wrong note played during a concert or struggling to remember the answers to high school matriculation examination questions. Everyone has faced situations where they would rather have been like SM. Of course, life would be easier if one could stay curious, active, capable and stress free in difficult situations. Nevertheless, most of us would still not want to be emotionless. Even experts studying fear do not want to be fearless.

The case of SM is well documented and known among fear researchers, so I asked fear researcher Schiller whether she wanted to be fearless like SM. After a short pause, Schiller said no. She said that, from an evolutionary point of view, what we started out with was pure reflexes. Then our prefrontal cortex developed on top of these automatic mechanisms. Now these two are engaged in a constant struggle to see whether the victor is our innate reactions to events or our ability to control them. It seems that, according to Schiller, fear and our struggle against it in some way define human beings as a species. Even though she may sometimes be annoyed at being afraid, she would still not choose a fearless life.

Being almost completely fearless might be beneficial at some areas of life, but there is always a trade off. In SM's case, she is the one to carry the heaviest price for her fearlessness. But there is another group of people who are almost as fearless as SM, but in their case the price is mostly borne by the people around them. Fearlessness is not as rare as people think it is, as almost one in a hundred are part of this group, that we sometime wish we wouldn´t have encountered at all.

4.

You may have met someone who at first seems charming. He is intelligent, charismatic, creative, extremely good at communicating, and apparently able to keep his cool in situations that make other people freeze up. However, in the long term you start to get bothered by the fact that he is able to maintain eye contact for longer than normal without blinking and that he does not seem to have a lot of friends. At some point, you may notice how effortlessly he manipulates the people around him. One day, you find out that he has lied about a number of things. When you stop to look at the evidence, you release that he seems to be an almost compulsive liar. Business is business for him, and morality is expendable. He knows neither shame nor regret, even when normal people would.[185]

These people are called psychopaths or sociopaths.[186] Or, to be more precise, they have an antisocial personality disorder.

Psychopaths in movies are portrayed as coldblooded criminals. Nevertheless, even though 15-25% of prison inmates in Finland are psychopaths, not all psychopaths are violent or criminals. Many of them become leaders, lawyers, media

---

185 Babiak P., Neumann, C.S., Hare R.D., "Corporate psychopathy: Talking the walk." *Behav Sci Law*. 2010 Mar-Apr; 28(2): 174–193. This study, like others, confirms that psychopaths are often found to be charismatic, creative, good communicators and strategic thinkers. However, they get low scores for responsibility, teamwork, leadership skills and general ability.

186 Psychologist Tuija Matikka writes aptly on the difference between psychopaths and sociopaths in the *Tiede* (2007) magazine: "Sociopaths are unlike psychopaths in that they do not betray everyone. A sociopath's indifferent behaviour is connected to his or her culture. For example, a Mafioso may ruthlessly kill members of a rival clan, but will loyally look after his own family."

personalities, salesmen, surgeons, journalists, policemen and cooks.[187]

One percent of human beings have the personality traits that define psychopathy. In other words, if you walk down the street and meet the eyes of a hundred bypassers, your hundredth eye contact will be with a psychopath. The frightening, fortunate or surprising (take your pick) thing is that the number of psychopaths in leadership positions is triple this number. If you work in an organization with a hundred managers, three of them, on average, will have the world's most infamous personality disorder.[188] Psychopaths appear to have abilities through which these people, who are incapable of empathy and manipulate their colleagues to nervous breakdowns, ascend to positions of high responsibility in the corporate world.

What are these abilities? Kevin Dutton, with a PhD in psychology – and whose own father is a psychopath – gives one answer in *The Wisdom of Psychopaths*. According to Dutton, psychopaths combine a strong personality with an unflagging ability to concentrate. They are able to act charming and to ignore distractions. They are ruthless, and what is more, fearless. It helps them to maintain their capacity to operate in even the most extreme situations. For this reason, psychopaths are over-represented in dangerous and difficult professions, where fear would normally wreck a person's ability to perform or would lead to high levels of distress.

---

187 This list can be found in Kevin Dutton's *The Wisdom of Psychopaths*, and is originally from the Great British Psychopath Survey.

188 Babiak P., Neumann, C.S., Hare R.D., "Corporate psychopathy: Talking the walk." *Behav Sci Law.* 2010 Mar-Apr; 28(2): 174–193.

The personality features inherent to psychopaths are highly valued in working life, as the mental qualities of psychopaths help them to manage in difficult situations time after time, without any negative effect on their performance. A machine is a machine, and feels nothing. However, unlike machines, some psychopaths like to play mind games – which is apparently the only area in which they experience fear. They are afraid of losing control and of having their true selves revealed. You can be sure that a psychopath will do anything in order to avoid having their control challenged when it comes to these things.

Just like with SM, psychopaths have, according to researchers, deficiencies in their amygdalas. On the other hand, these deficiencies are different than with SM, who had suffered damage to that part of her brain. Psychopaths have smaller amygdalas than healthy people, but more importantly, there is a difference in the amount of white matter in their brains, i.e., the substance that connects the various parts of one's brain. It is like a highway connecting the different areas of the brain. Psychopaths appear to have less white matter between the amygdala and those parts of the brain responsible for inhibiting behaviour.[189] They do not learn from frightening experiences, and their amygdalas do not become active in situations where they normally would. Consequently, these people are in high demand in management positions. This should surprise nobody: after all, who among us has not wished that someone would stay calm in a confusing situation, someone who seems to know what to do.

---

189 This is quite evidently the only area in which they have less, as an excess of white matter is often connected with pathological lying.

Psychopathic leaders are not guided by their emotions, because in practice they have none.

So much for the upsides. As already mentioned, psychopathic leaders are rarely the ones who end up bearing the cost of fear – that cost falls on those around them. The estimate according to which three per cent of people in leadership positions are psychopaths is based on personality tests conducted with 203 managers. Even though this proportion may seem high, it intuitively seems easy to accept. Those people who shamelessly manipulate other people, are unafraid of the consequences of taking extreme risks, and do not feel sorry for what they do can rise high in the halls of power. There are two reasons for this. First of all, some psychopaths do a great job, and do not cause harm to society or their environment. We are for example ready to pay in order for someone to represent us in a difficult court case, and want to see leaders who act calmly in crisis situations and remain functional even in the middle of a catastrophe. For that matter, few of us would want to be operated on by an emotionally volatile surgeon. We need steady hands, not someone who really gets our inner self. Yes, they can be extremely good at what they are doing, but they present a great threat for any feeling of security inside the company.

The other reason is more sinister: we do not, on the whole, stop psychopaths from doing their thing. The overrepresentation of psychopaths in leading positions in a company may be due to corporate structure or culture. Psychopaths seem to do particularly well in companies where people are raised to management positions based on personality, rather than results, and where transparency is low. For a psychopath, devoid of conscience, this kind of corporation is ripe for the picking. However, if a company emphasises transparency, promotes strong values and promotes employees based on performance, there is little room for psychopaths to manoeuvre.

5.

Psychopaths can be extremely good at certain jobs and tasks. Nevertheless, even if one were to consider this a good thing, there is something fundamentally wrong about the rise of these people to the professional elite of certain professions. I do not believe that we want to create the kind of jobs or corporations where only completely emotionless people excel. The inability of psychopaths for empathy and experiencing fear easily leads to collateral damage to the people around them. The risk is particularly great when psychopaths are hired to a workplace and then promoted. Through their behaviour, they erode the trust between the people in a given community, and cause problems for everyone through their amoral behaviour. A person who is unafraid of shame or punishments is easily capable of that. Up to a point, shareholders may consider the means irrelevant, so long as shareholder value increases. But they are far from meaningless for those who have to actually work in the company.

According to a study done in Australia, bullying at the workplace increases when psychopaths are working there, and decreases when they are not present. This one-percenter gang[190] was responsible for over 25% of all workplace bullying cases.

---

190 In this study, the number of psychopaths in the work community was approximately 1%, which is to say the average amount in the general population.

Psychopaths who had reached positions of leadership treated their employees unfairly and were completely indifferent to their feelings.[191]

Psychopaths do well in a corporate culture based on fear, and complex and opaque organizational structures serve to protect them. The only way to get rid of this distortion is to take away their protection by promoting maximum transparency in all activities, by curbing excesses and by endorsing humane corporate values, values that are not to be ignored.

Even though fear has a cost, complete fearlessness also seems to have a cost. It seems that by removing our fears (and the connected structures), we also remove some part of what makes us human. Psychopathological emotionlessness mixes up one's moral compass and leaves behind an emotionless over-performer, for whom other people are just tools. And even though SM, despite being fearless, had an otherwise wide variety of emotions, she still had trouble maintaining social relationships.

As Daniela Schiller stated concerning SM: if you remove fear, you remove one of the more interesting parts of life. Which is to say the interplay between ancient defence mechanisms and the newer layers of the brain that control them – i.e., beating yourself.

Even though one should not and cannot remove fear partly or in whole, there are still many different ways of controlling fear's harmful effects, or in some cases completely bypassing them.

---

191 Boddy, C.R., "Corporate Psychopaths, Bullying and Unfair Supervision in the Workplace," Journal of Business Ethics, 2011, Volume 100, Issue 3, pp 367–379.

Corporate Rhapsody

1.

Farrokh Bulsara, a Zanzibarian performer, recorded a song that he had composed and written, a song that was in many ways problematic. For one thing, the song looked like it would be impossible to record using the studio technology available at the time. The song included innumerable variations and sections, which could only be recorded using clever overdubbing.

In the 1970s, albums were made analogically and manually. If you wanted to change or shorten the sections of a song, you had to physically cut the tape.[192] If you needed to add more tracks, you had to copy the master tape, freeing new tracks for use. Every time the tape was wound back or forth, the pick ups wore away at it. According to the wildest legends relating to the recordings, the master tape for Bulsara's work wore so thin that you could see through it, and with its many cuts it looked like there was a zebra crossing on the tape reel. Recording the song pushed the studio technicians professionally and mentally to their limits.

Moreover, the technical challenges were a minor detail compared to the other difficulties relating to the song. The final work was almost 6 minutes long, and depending on how you looked at it, featured two or three different genres. That was unacceptable in the 1970s. Radio stations simply refused to play songs that

---

192 For you digital natives: songs used to be recorded, not figuratively but literally, with every sound recorded on a physical tape, a little like a big C cassette without a plastic case.

long. The ideal length of a single was 3 minutes and 30 seconds. The songs that got the most airtime had either originally been composed for that length, had been recorded at that length or the record company had made a new radio version of the long version.

In addition, the genres were problematic. Paul Watts, the director responsible for publishing Bulsara's albums was convinced that BBC Radio One, the radio channel that was most important for the potential commercial success of the album, would absolutely refuse to play the song. He demanded that a shorter and more straightforward single version of the song be produced. Bulsara refused. What would you have done?

Let us first look at things from the point of view of the record company director. He was given a recording that breached at least two of the most important rules he had learned during his professional career. The radio stations were the ones who created hits, so in order to get a hit, you had to play by their rules. You could get airtime if your song had a clear hook, i.e., a distinctive refrain, and had the sound typical for the period, i.e., was similar to other songs on the radio. Bulsara's recording seems almost like a parody with its shifts in genres – even though no one has been able to say what it would be a parody of. In addition, the recording company director knew that, historically, only those songs have gotten airtime that comply with the above rules, and in addition the golden rule relating to the length of a hit single. We must also bear in mind the stakes: publishing an album is a financial risk. Which one would have been more sensible: to let Bulsara do what he wanted or to demand that he make a more radio friendly version?

Let us next look at Bulsara's problem. His career is looking fairly good, but he still has not managed a breakthrough. He is charismatic and his band shows promise, but they have few die-hard fans and most of the band's bigger gigs have been warming up for more popular bands. The band has just managed to get rid of a bad record company, and the boss of the new company is not excited about Bulsara's latest work of art. When he plays the new song to the general manager of the record company, he throws a fit, saying these exact words: "What the fuck's this? Are you mad?" Bulsara also plays the song for a fellow artist he respects, whose first comment is likewise: "Are you fucking mad?" Bulsara is in a situation where the sacred rules of the music business are against him, his colleague thinks that his band is a group of nutjobs and the boss of his own record company thinks that the song is unpublishable and messed up. What's more, the friend he played the song to for the first time burst out laughing. This is the situation in which Bulsara has to make his choice: either to eat humble pie, clean up the unnecessary little flourishes from his song and cut it to a radio friendly length, or to keep his head and refuse to make any changes, demanding that the song be published as a single without any changes.

Bulsara made his choice, and the song became one of the most recognizable and widely sold hits of all time. You have almost certainly heard it. Farrokh Bulsara is better known as Freddie Mercury, and the band is Queen. The song is Bohemian Rhapsody, which went on to become one of the strangest, most high selling, and infectious megahits in the history of rock and roll. The song was released in its original form and length, according to the wishes of Freddie and his band. The public loved it. The week it came out, Bohemian Rhapsody rose to number 47 on the British singles list. About a week later, it was number 17, then 9, and finally number #1 on the official UK singles list. Bohemian

Rhapsody went on to become the third highest selling single in Britain of all time.

With a number one hit single, Queen stepped into the limelight – for good. Queen was on everyone's lips, and you could not avoid hearing Mercury's "bismillahs" and "scara mus." It was a song that people felt strongly about. Of course, some also laughed at or hated Bohemian Rhapsody, but that only gave more fuel to the public discussion around the band and propelled them to even greater fame.

It is easy to dismiss the story of the Bohemian Rhapsody as yet another anecdote behind a great classic, but there is a greater, everyday lesson there. You have to make the characters a little less epic and compromise on the level of artistic creativity involved, but otherwise this same story is acted out at workplaces every day. Encountering an original idea is like finding a hairnet in one's soup; one's initial reaction is usually immediate and violent rejection. Gradually, ideas and the people who present them start to look alike, and the discussion becomes burdened with unwritten rules, which stifle original thinking. Bohemian Rhapsody was immediately seized upon by music industry professionals. The manager who wanted to shorten the song was Paul Allen, the international affairs rep of Queen's record company. The man who thought Freddy and his band were nuts was trusted artist friend Elton John.[193] Freddie Mercury had a novel view, weighing in at 5 minutes and 55 seconds, which contained a mismatched medley of contradicting genres: ballad, heavy metal and opera or something like opera. Against all expectations, he

---

193 Granted, based on his own appearance in the 1970s, he should have been in no position to criticise the artistic choices of others.

managed to get his way, and the song was released and rose to the top of the charts.

2.

One might not think that ordinary working people have much in common with Freddie Mercury. His charisma was known to keep the audience enthralled, just like Fidel Castro and his famous stadium speeches, with the exception that people who walked out of a Queen concert midway through were not likely to face serious repercussions. However, Freddie was faced with the same challenges that have stood in the way of every original idea throughout the ages.

Brain scientist and neuroeconomist Gregory Berns believes that fears are a key obstacle to creativity. According to Berns, fear reactions in particular are decisive in many ways. It is not enough to hatch an original idea and to think about it, but one must in the end subject it to evaluation by others. The threat of failure, being in an unfamiliar situation and the ridicule – or mere expectation thereof – of others trigger those parts of the brain relating to defence reactions.[194] Fear of failure is often followed, as we have seen, by running away from situations or trying to avoid them. It is a logical reaction, as stored fear memories automatically direct us to avoid future dangers. A person quickly learns the pain of failure, which can by itself be enough for him to keep all unconventional ideas to himself. In the time

---

194 Berns, G., Iconoclast. *A Neuroscientist Reveals How to Think Differently,* 2008.

honoured words of John Maynard Keynes: "Worldly wisdom teaches that it is better for reputation to fail conventionally than to succeed unconventionally."

Freddie Mercury refused to submit to his fears and to water down his idea so that his bandmates and the record company would accept it without qualms. After all, it would have been quite simple to do so. If Mercury had removed the operatic parts of the song, it would have been easy and effortless to sell the song to his bandmates and the record company.

The song ended up on an album and as a single on the radio almost solely due to Mercury's creativity, stubbornness and one influential radio DJ. That is to say, not all of Freddie's nearest and dearest shared the views of the record company and Elton John. BBC One weekend DJ Kenny Everett was enthralled by the song.[195] At first he played excerpts of the song on his show, and finally the whole piece – a total of fourteen times during one weekend. At this point, the record company could no longer claim that BBC would refuse to play the song. Furthermore, Everett's tour de force put further pressure on the record company to agree to a release, as already on Monday people were going to record stores to ask for the song they had heard on Everett's program.[196] EMI caved.

It is useless to speculate about how successful Queen would have been without Bohemian Rhapsody. For that, we would need a Queen living in a parallel universe, one which would have

---

195 For digital natives: back in the day, a radio DJ could turn a song into a breakout hit by playing it just once on the radio

196 For digital natives: record stores used to be the places to purchases these 7- and 12-inch recordings, long before Napster and high-speed internet killed both the stores and the physical records they were selling.

knuckled under and agreed to the changes. However, I think it is safe to say that this song is a keystone of Queen's music and helped the band reach sales of 300 million records.

Moreover, what is more important than the effects of the song is to understand what kind of risk Mercury took in standing up for his views. The UK singles lists supported Paul Watts' view. There was no indication whatsoever that a 6-minute heavy-ballad-mock-opera combination would be well received. Had Mercury been wrong, he would have sealed his fate. Paul Watts would have been proved right, and the song would have at most been played on radio programmes dedicated to musical oddities, helped along by the disparaging laughter of radio DJs.[197]

The story of the *Bohemian Rhapsody* makes one think about just how many original ideas have been watered down or destroyed in the companies in which we work. Would the song ever have been published, if Queen had been like an average company in terms of its atmosphere and product development processes?

3.

Risk and business are inseparably connected. The rule of thumb is that the bigger the risk, the greater the profit you can and should expect. The smartest business people look for risks where the risk is limited but the profits are limitless – in other words

---

197 Of course, now we can laugh at Paul Watts' lack of vision and be thankful that the song ended up with Mike Myers and Dana Carwey going on to produce the greatest lip-synching and head-banging scene of all time in *Wayne's World*.

situations where you can lose your stake without it breaking you, but where success can bring almost endless profits.[198] However, in practice most business seems to be about obsessively removing risks, rather than looking for opportunities where the risks are limited and the profits unlimited.

Risk avoidance has become something of an art and a science for companies,[199] which includes ordering unnecessary studies, delaying decisions, diluting radical ideas, outsourcing one's thinking to consultants, relegating decision making to the top tiers of the company, using political rhetoric and engaging in endless meetings, where any new and brave ideas are deflated. These behaviours and models are fear-based, even though some might call them business as usual.

It is easy to spot fear in its different corporate forms: in endless studies that never produce any new thinking, managers afraid to say anything that might mean something, bureaucracy, approval procedures, stiff R&D models and a SYA (save your ass) mentality at the workplace, market studies and reports that are used by decision makers purely to cover their own backs. When it is time to find a fall guy, it helps to have an almost "academic" safety pillow on the floor that one can sit on and show that even though failure was painful, no mistakes were made.

According to one provocative estimate, 80% of the 40 billion USD[200] used on market research globally every year produces nothing new. In other words, 32 billion dollars are used every

---

198 Here I draw on the ideas of Nassim N. Taleb, though cautiously, as based on his Twitter feed no one has, to date, understood correctly anything he has said. However, I refuse to borrow an idea without quoting the source.

199 The only thing that some companies make an art out of.

200 Global Market Research 2014, An ESOMAR Industry Report.

year in order to deal with fear. It is hard to say whether this kind of estimate holds any water, but it is interesting to think about to what extent we really focus on exploring new possibilities and to what extent we just concentrate on trying to save our asses.

Fear can be found in visions and strategies that include everything under the sun– which at the same time means that they say nothing at all. Consequently, no one can be caught out due to something they said or a mistake they made. "Our strategy aims for sustainable, profitable growth over the long-term. In the short-term, we are focusing on improving our competitiveness and cash flow and on securing our profitability. This means continuous improvement of our operations – productivity, operational excellence, quality and cost competitiveness." In other words, this company has set, as a goal, precisely what every public company should be doing in any case. On the other hands, it demonstrates some integrity that the corporation is brave enough to admit that they are not concerned, in the short or the long term, with their customers, employees, or in fact anything else except money.[201]

---

201 The excerpt in the book is from the company's old strategy. Here is the new one: "Our aim is to strengthen and expand our leading market positions in our core businesses in order to achieve faster-than-market growth and improved profitability. The unique combination of equipment, services and intelligence in our existing offering can deliver customer value propositions that improve customers' operational efficiency, safety, sustainability and cost effectiveness over the life cycle. These elements can be supplied to our customers through our standard or value-based business models, either as stand-alone offerings or as different types of combinations. Our strategic ambition is to become the leading process performance provider for our customers to enable them to achieve sustainable process improvements. Our capabilities and our market-leading businesses and technologies put us in a unique position to realise this ambition. The core of this strategy as an intelligent processes and services company is based on the ability to create significant and sustainable customer value by combining and integrating our core equipment, services and intelligence. The Metso advantage is based on owning products, services, skills and technologies that are robust and market-tested also

It is in a way endearing that something so deeply embedded in human nature as fear can have such a strong influence on strategy, which is the bedrock of a company. The greatest paradox of fear is that in human history, fear has had (and of course still has) a life-preserving role, but in business, fear leads to decay, degeneration or death.[202] It turns companies into the living dead, organisations where the only task of employees is to climb as high as they can on the power ladder of corporate politics, and to look for risk-free methods, such as cutting costs and making cuts in order to improve shareholder value.

Just a few words of warning before we look at examples to the contrary. Avoiding risks is not automatically risk free, and taking risks does not automatically lead to success. The fundamental flaw in success stories is how linear they are. This is because success stories are always written after the fact. When you look back, it seems like all of your diverse choices inevitably led to a certain result. What success stories neglect to mention are the fates of thousands (or millions) of entrepreneurs who, despite making the same choices, did not end up on the front pages of business magazines.[203] For example, Dutch composer

---

on a stand-alone basis. Strategic must-wins. With the need to embed even more intelligence into machines, services and processes, we have adjusted our must-win agenda and its priorities. We will highlight the equipment and intelligent solutions much more in the future. Our strategy implementation will continue based on five Group-level must-wins (Services, Technology offering, Growth countries, Operational excellence, People and leadership)." Did your heart skip a beat reading all that?

202 Healthy fear can of course stir growth in a company. For example, if salespersons treat customers arrogantly, R&D fails to notice competitors sprint past and future changes do not promote new kinds of thinking, then the same result follows, i.e., the decay and death of the company.

203 I understand that the success stories in this book are in the same category. However, I do not mean to say that for example acting like coach Iain Dowie would

John Ewbank combined choral song, rap and string instruments in Koningslied, i.e., The King's Song,.. However, in the end he retracted his song due to the public mockery that had been directed at it. For every Bohemian Rhapsody there are countless Koninglieds, but that's the whole point. We intuitively recognise the risk of failure, but submitting to it never leads to anything new, just more bland and colourless corporate stagnation. It is far more interesting to look at those people and companies that take risks, deciding against the odds to operate in a different way.

<h2 style="text-align:center">4.</h2>

BrewDog, a Scottish brewery, shipped a beer in July 2010 that inflamed the social media and aggravated animal rights organizations and alcohol advertising regulators. The specialty beer was called The End of History, and was at the time the strongest beer in the world, ABV 55%. Moreover, not only was the beer the most alcoholic, it was also the most expensive. One bottle cost either 500 or 700 pounds, depending on how it was packaged. A beer wrapped in a stoat weighed in at 500 pounds, while one wrapped in a grey squirrel cost an extra 200 pounds. Yes, the beers were wrapped in animals that had died in traffic accidents.[204]

---

always inevitably lead to success, but rather that this kind of method provides the opportunity for success.

204 A professional taxidermist had stitched the bottles inside animals that had died as roadkill. When I asked James Watt what packing option they turned down, he answered: shark, as few would have a large enough shelf for it Given that this was BrewDog, I was unsure whether this was a joke or whether they had really considered sharks.

The End of History was, as a beer, such a maverick product that it simply could not be over-looked. One either loved or hated it – indifference was not an option. And that was precisely what brewery founders Martin Dickie and James Watt wanted. Everyone reacted to the product: animal rights activists, the body responsible for self regulation of alcohol companies, and of course the media. Critics felt that the stunt was a tasteless, stupid marketing gimmick, a violation of good marketing practice, and cruelty against animals. Even though Watt admits that the reaction was rather violent, it was still incredible to witness it. They had aimed to cause a shock, and that they certainly did. The End of History brought BrewDog to the limelight. The product itself was mentioned 10,000 times on Twitter, and the article by BBC on the beer was the most shared item for two days. The product also featured on the lists of most read articles on CNN and Fox News. During the week after release, the beer got BrewDog about 650,000 pounds worth of media coverage.[205]

Even if one does not approve of BrewDog's campaign, one has to admit that it was more than just a marketing stunt. It is a good example of the kind of jackpot you can win if you dare to take a risk. BrewDog has been a maverick from the day it was founded, and done things that, to conventional sense, seemed to make no sense. Watt and Dickie founded the company in 2007 on their savings and a bank loan. They had gotten fed up with their jobs, the corporate cultures of their workplaces and in particular with the dull and uninspired beers they brewed.

---

205 BrewDog is competing against giant breweries and their marketing budgets, and therefore BrewDog has to rise above the noise created by these megabreweries and to do something unusual in order to get its message through. Watt claims that, due to these giant breweries, consumers have less choice. This is probably true.

To Watt and Dickie, none of the beers on the market had any taste, and more importantly, there was no beer brand for their generation, the punk generation. Dickie, who had studied the art of brewing, and Watt built their first brewery, manufactured their first products in their garage and started selling their products at fairs. They gained fans steadily, but the first major turning point for their business came when their beers took the fourth, third, second and first place at the 2008 Tesco Drink Awards. After that, Tesco ordered 20,000 cases of beer a week and BrewDog was on its way.

But it was the End of History and the preceding contest with the German Schorschbrau brewery for the title of strongest beer in the world that really made BrewDog and its beers famous worldwide.

According to Watt, the core of, and the basis for what they do is passion for beer and the making thereof. "Passion sounds like such a simple thing, but the thing is that that's what separates the winners from the losers."[206] BrewDog may be a small challenger on the enormous beverage market, but it is steadily becoming a good sized company, even on an international scale. BrewDog is valued at 30 million pounds, with annual revenue of approximately 30 million pounds. The company has been growing at a staggering rate the last five years.

BrewDog has become a company that reaps success in a conservative industry by taking huge risks. Or in any case, that is what it looks like from the outside. However, if one takes a closer look, one may get a different view. They took a small risk with "The End of History." In practice, the worst case scenario was that the

---

206 Watt's comments from correspondence between 22 and 29 July 2014.

release of the beer would have been followed by complete silence. It would have meant writing off the production costs and the time spent developing the beer. However, even these would not have been a complete loss, as they would have learned something during the project. The company's future prospects could have become significantly bleaker if the buying public had abandoned Brew-Dog's other products due to a media furore. This was a possibility, but a rather unlikely one, as even if things had turned out badly, they could always have apologised. Even if "The End of History" would have irrevocably destroyed the reputation of BrewDog, at least the guys would have had a good story to tell. I do not wish to sound pathetic, but I think time spent with their own company would probably have in any case beaten the other option, which is that Watt and Dickie would have stuck with the mind-numbing corporate jobs they had before founding BrewDog.

These are not the kinds of options that Watt and Dickie need to look at for now, as BrewDog has been a phenomenal success. Moreover, though there are almost 300 people working for BrewDog, it is showing no signs of stagnation. BrewDog is still making products that are so unique and distinctive that they market themselves. BrewDog's latest came out of in a few selected countries: the "Hello My Name Is…" beer. The citizens of the selected countries could vote on the names of the beer. In Russia, the beer was named "Putin." After unveiling the name, one of the founding members of BrewDog gave a statement, according to which the beer was not meant for gays. And this comment was not aimed at homosexuals.

BrewDog may have no other choice but to make products that sell themselves. According to James Watt, he would rather take his money and set fire to it than use it on conventional marketing. According to Watt, they still hold true to this principle, having spent not a pound on conventional advertising.

5.

BrewDog seems to be fighting against the most common pattern in growth companies. This pattern is as follows. A group of enthusiastic entrepreneurs starts to do something they care about, and finds success. Their success is followed by hiring "professionals," as the founders are only interested in fulfilling their original idea, which is an art of its own. After that, more professionals start flooding into the company. They bring with them their models, spreadsheets, risk analyses and processes. The company starts to do things "sensibly," and the time and energy of the employees is increasingly spent on meetings, reporting, asking for permission and serving the needs of the organisation. At the top of the company, power is taken away from those who are interested in exceptional products and customer experiences, and given to those who are primarily interested in money. Finally, the passion is gone and so is any hint of courage, and what the customers get is lifeless products and joyless service.

This gradual loss of courage seems almost like a law of nature. However, it does not necessarily need to be. Courage and originality only disappear if the company's values consist of something less than an almost fanatical obsession with whatever it is that the company does. According to Watt of BrewDog, "The End of History" was in a nutshell their way of making controversial art.[207] If your choices are determined by money, corporate politics, shareholder value, risk avoidance or personal reputation, you will face completely different risks than when your core value is that the people working at the company should do something they are proud of. Of course, that is not easy or risk free either.[208] One wrong choice can lead to huge losses of money or reputation. Failure, misunderstanding, mockery and attention can sometimes feel unpleasant. One feels ashamed or anxious, or gets butterflies in the belly.

The problem with the corporate spirit[209] is that it lacks this kind of dedication. The primary task of corporations is not to do something exceptional but to produce value for their owners. This does not necessarily have to be the case, but it is how things are. This may be due to the things that companies focus on. With BrewDog, the founders seemed to be more interested in the product than in money: handmade beer. Watt and Dickie have never told the world that they mainly think of shareholder value. What they want to tell people about is their passion for beer.

What a company is interested in means a great deal. If a company is interested in many things, then paradoxically enough it is not actually interested in anything in particular. Decision making becomes difficult if those who are involved in making decisions do not have a clear view of what is essential. For example, a company can announce that they are interested in a corporate culture

---

207 One bottle of The End of History ended up in the Mona museum in Australia

208 It is almost impossible to rise above this. Entrepreneurs, corporate directors and corporate artists are limited by fears that also limit me. These fears are not easily bypassed.

209 I use the term corporate spirit, as this same lack of dedication and focus can trouble even the smallest corporations.

where employees' happiness is key.[210] This affects the choices the company makes, like whether it instructs employees to book flights with many transfers, as these are cheaper, or finds another way of saving money and lets employees book direct flights, so that they can get home to their families and children faster.

To simplify, one could probably find a company's key interest in the following list: shareholder value, management bonuses and promotions, revenue, the product and/or service, the people who work for the company, or a larger cause. None of these are bad or illegal per se. However, a company where the prime focus is on shareholder value is a very different place to work than one where the main focus is on producing high quality, original products (BrewDog), people's happiness (Zappos) or removing global poverty (The Grameen Bank). Moreover, it is not just for small companies or start ups.

Multibillionaire Elon Musk is one of those who emphasise passion and meaning. Musk is the owner of electric car company Tesla, solar power producer SolarCity, and reusable spaceship manufacturer SpaceX. In an interview with Forbes, he has said that the main thing that has brought him success is that he does things he is passionate about, but that are at the same time useful to other.[211] According to a 2008 survey by consulting firms O.C. Tanner and TowersPerrin, the same seems to hold true not just for the owners but for everyone in the company. Employees want their work to have a clear meaning.[212] When

---

210 For example, online store Zappos is one such company.

211 Clash, J., "Elon Musk tells me his secret of success," Forbes 28.7.2014

212 *The Orange Revolution* by Adrian Gostick and Chester Elton mentions the results of The Global Recognition Study. This study was commissioned by O.C. Tanner, with 10,333 people interviewed in 13 countries for them.

employees are proud of their job, they become more committed to the company's goals and their own tasks. But most importantly clearly communicated meaning (what the company is interested about) creates trust and even passion.[213] And trust is naturally an antidote for fear. Companies that tend to focus mainly and foremost on making money or building shareholder value usually miss this completely.

However, not everyone wants to test their limits or to leave their mark on the world. Corporations are a great place to hide for those who do not want to do something original, significant or dangerous. And, as we will soon see, corporations are also sometimes madhouses for those who want to make decisions.

6.

Imagine for a moment that you are working as a manager at a global company. You are responsible for a fairly large business area. One day, you notice that one of your employees has fallen into a salary pit. She joined the firm as an intern, and gradually worked her way up in the organisation to a position of responsibility. She got the standard annual pay raises, but still got left behind in comparison to the salaries of her colleagues. Now she is responsible for a business unit with revenue in the tens of millions of euros, and her salary does not match her current

---

213 However, passion is often misunderstood. Passion is not a euphoric feeling of excitement, but rather a continuing source of motivation. Personally, I feel that real passion is always connected to learning. Learning is a part of one's life that is always rewarding and feeds itself. Therefore, its effects extend beyond momentary extremes of emotion, and for example help to deal with periods of slow progress that one inevitably faces time and again in one's hobbies, work and business.

position. You decide to fix things. You tell your employee about the situation, and she replies that she has gotten an offer from a competing company, and intends to leave the company. You ask her to reconsider, and promise to deal with it – after all, it is only a 600-euro monthly raise. She agrees to wait, and you make a proposal for a raise. A good employee, quite possibly a future key employee is leaving, and you have the opportunity to stop this. It is a modest raise, even when looking at her annual salary. Here we come to the old joke: how many managers does it take to make a decision about a few hundred euro pay raise?

A manager called MP[214] ended up in precisely this kind of situation while working in a multinational ICT company. In his view, the situation was critical. He absolutely did not want to lose a good employee, and that employee's present salary was by no means fair when considering her abilities and proven results.[215] However, MP immediately realised that he did not have the authority to make such a decision, even though he was the director of that business unit. On the other hand, this is standard practice in many big companies. They adhere to a one up policy, i.e., the decision is taken to the person who is the supervisor of the one who made the proposal. In this case, this person was the country manager of the company. However, the country manager found out that this kind of decision exceeded his authority as well. The proposal was kicked up the ladder. Next, the directors at the Nordic manager level noticed that, even though the room was full of genial Swedes, business-savvy Danes, and cod- and raw oil-infused Norwegians, they could

---

214 Who preferred to remain anonymous.

215 Yes, this was a woman.

not make such a decision – they simply did not have the power. They had to kick the decision up to the EMEA[216] evel – in vain. The decision turned out to be so important to the company that even EMEA-level directors were not competent enough to make that decision and it had to be made by the global headquarters. The upside is, someone in California was finally able to make the decision – they said yes. The employee was given a pay raise of 600 euros per month. Unfortunately, the damage was already done. Both the employee and the employee's supervisor, who had originally proposed the pay raise, left the company. The supervisor said that management requires making decisions. In a company where decisions are only made at global headquarters, a manager's title is just a joke. So, to answer the question of how many managers (and organisations) it takes to make a decision on a few hundred euros: at least five, on two different continents.

7.

Oh the frustration, when competent and reasonably intelligent people are treated as incompetent and untrust-worthy. A notice pops up on my screen, telling me that I do not have the rights to do what I am trying to do. I need to ask a higher authority, the administrator, for permission. I have never met the administrator, but I have heard his voice. Of course, the administrator does sound different every time I call. But he is the administrator, and I have to adjust my own actions to his rules and his changing voice. I cannot question his actions, because he is supported

---

216 Europe, Middle-East and Africa.

by a higher authority or power, which is called data security. I pick up the receiver and dial the number provided. A young man answers the phone, and I explain my situation. He listens sympathetically to my problem, and then tells me he is going to remotely seize my computer. This sounds like something out of Close Encounters of the Third Kind, but I go along with it.

I am still on the phone, and something starts to happen on my screen. The bar on my screen for data transfer tells me that the necessary update is currently being downloaded onto my hard-drive. I thank the administrator, and end the call. The program finishes downloading. I close it, following the instructions popping up on my screen, and open it again. Now I have the newest version of iTunes,[217] along with a side helping of anxiety. It took me almost half an hour from when I first pressed the "update" button.

The first few times, wasting your working time creates powerful feelings of aggressions. Gradually, this anger is dulled and turns into a kind of overall dissatisfaction that gnaws at your motivation somewhere on a subconscious level. Eventually, over time, you turn into a corporate zombie.

Economist and sociologist Max Weber wrote that one of the qualities of a bureaucracy is the removal of mistakes. It is, however, an utopian ideal so long as there are people involved.[218] Nevertheless, various models based on the fear of mistakes still try to eliminate mistakes. But do they succeed in removing all

---

217 For digital natives: iTunes is a music store from which we, who are used to buying albums, can still buy and own our own copies.

218 I have heard that the data centres of big IT firms work at almost 100% availability, but only when people are not involved. Indeed, it seems that as a result of information technology and robotics, the only thing at which man is better than machine is in making mistakes.

errors? Perhaps, but at what price? What if the cost of mistakes has been exaggerated, and at the same time another cost is forgotten: the cost of teaching employees that the system bears all responsibility or that employees have no power over the things they are supposed to be responsible for.

8.

Enforcing policies on, and transferring power over decision making to the highest level in a company may sometimes be necessary, but there is always a cost. Increasing bureaucracy and concentrating power at the top is the laziest possible way of thinking for a company's directors – and sends the strongest possible signals. The directors of the company are sending a message that they earn their high salaries by making petty decisions all day and confirming the expenses filings of their underlings. By doing this, they are unequivocally telling the lower rungs of the corporate ladder that they are not trusted.

Over-controlling due to fear can be justified on the basis of various risks. However, these risks tend to be exaggerated. What are people afraid of in these organisations? Are they afraid that a to all appearances sensible person, once given some responsibility, will immediately go nuts, take the company credit card, and order a million euros worth of navel warmers? And that this same fear holds true for all employees?

Maybe we need new ways to think about risk and building trust in workplaces. The problem is, on the face of it there are few examples to the contrary, because the conventional wisdom of senior management and management consultants is to use various governance models loaded with distrust and worst case scenarios, while these people have very little experience of what actually happens when a company acts in such a way that it shows its employees they are trusted. Fortunately, we do have some examples, such as Futurice (two time winner of Great Place to Work Europe's No 1 Small & Medium Workplace), an IT company operating in Finland, Germany and the UK. Futurice took a risk – and profited. Every employee at the firm has a company credit card. Purchases do not need to be confirmed with a supervisor, and every card user only has two conditions: receipts must be sent to accounting for the taxman, and when making a purchase, the employee has to think about what effect it will have on colleagues, clients and the company in both the short and the long term. In other words, this is a mutually agreed way of using money, rather than a means of control. If a company card holder decides, based on these criteria, that the purchase would be a good idea, he or she just goes ahead and does it. There is no need to ask for permission or to write justifications anywhere. No one is going to come asking about the decision afterward, because the employee is trusted.

The company's practices are completely transparent. All credit card purchases are open for assessment by colleagues. However, according to Hanno Nevanlinna, cultural director of Futurice, no one goes over other employees decisions due to the amount of purchases. The company's shared value is trust, and colleagues trust that others will make good 3 x 2 decisions.

According to Nevanlinna, the practice was started in 2008, when the management of Futurice decided that the conventional model of confirming expenses was impractical. They decided to transfer power of decision to those who needed the decisions.

At the same time, they decided to accept trust as one of their key management principles. Nevanlinna has stated that a practice whereby travel expenses had to be confirmed afterward had started to feel foolish.

It would be justified to assume that there would have been at least a few abuses of this policy over the years. However, it turns out that no such thing has happened. No one has bought up all the navel warmers on the market.[219] No one has betrayed the trust of the company. Nevanlinna admits that occasionally it turns out that people should have made different decisions, but that is hindsight. This is also part of showing trust. Colleagues trust that a decision was made based on the facts available at the time, and there is considerable pressure among colleagues to make good choices. If a decision seems good, the decision maker will discuss with the people concerned, or may even involve them in the decision making.

In addition, people wish to learn from decisions. The employees organise meetings in which they discuss the effects of choices made by employees, lessons learned and future plans. Employees also calculate opportunity costs. For example, how much would it cost if work were to be slowed down due to an inoperable tool, and how much it would help if they immediately acquired a newer version.

---

219 Futurice's expenses are in the same ballpark as those of other growth companies going international. We could also ask what would happen if someone did abuse a credit card. This is quite possible, and over a certain period even likely. However, this would only lead to a catastrophe if most of the company's employees simultaneously maxed out their credit cards. Which is rather unlikely.

The policy undertaken by Futurice management not to control their employees has resulted in employees thinking about decisions and their effects, because they are responsible for the consequences. Many managers desperately want responsible employees. Futurice has managed to create them by giving people power. In addition, the company believes that if employees are shown trust, they will feel valued. Trust affects employees' job satisfaction and dedication to their work. Futurice has twice been selected as the best place to work in Europe.[220]

Futurice is a growth company employing 300 people in three companies, but nothing is stopping bigger companies from adopting this practice. Jack Welch, legendary director of General Electric, also followed a similar policy, at least when it came to decision making. I talked to Welch at Nordic Business Forum (2013). Welch thinks that decisions should be made at the level that has the best knowledge for that particular decision. Welch had what can be described as a hostile attitude to bureaucracy. One of the company's values during his reign was eradicating bureaucracy. During his term, Welch cut out the many middle layers that had become established at GE. When Welch came to GE, there were 27 levels of management at the company. When he retired, there were only five. According to Welch, each layer slowed things down. It also reduced face-to-face communication, which is essential for Welch's model of leadership. According to Welch, a supervisor has two key tasks: to tell people where their careers are headed and what their supervisor thinks of their work

---

220 The Great Place to Work survey, 2012 and 2013. No other European workplace has achieved this.

at the company. According to Welch, this information should never be held back and then sprung on employees by surprise. Another important task is to get people excited. Or as Welch put it, to create an atmosphere of enthusiasm.

It may be surprising to hear that the general director of a multinational company, which was once the biggest in the world, felt the great size of his company to be the worst possible disadvantage. Welch speaks about "a big company's muscles" and "small company behaviour." According to Welch, it is immensely useful for a company to have the resources of a big firm but the culture of a small one. "Knowing the customer who comes in for the love of bread, knowing the family of the customer [...] You want that intimacy."[221]

Of course, it is true that there are some intellectually and socially challenging decisions to be made when you choose this path. Zappos, which employs thousands of people, has many practices, which embody their decision to choose trust rather than fear and control. CEO Tony Hsieh for example decided that the use of the company's library by employees would not be supervised, even though one of the employees was selling Zappos' books on eBay. Library cards and CCTVs would have probably solved the problem, but at the same time would have caused another one. Even though only one of the employees was bending the rules, the message for all others would have been clear: we don't trust any of you. Such supervision would have broken the trust between company management and employees.

---

221 Comments by Jack Welch from a discussion with him at a VIP Seminar of the Nordic Business Forum in Jyväskylä, Central Finland, on 25 September 2013 (our second discussion was at the actual Nordic Business Forum, on 27 September 2013).

Hsieh turned the whole thing into a small scale publicity stunt by having stickers attached to the books, indicating that the books had been provided by Zappos.

CEO Stephen M.R. Covey,[222] son of the late Stephen R. Covey, claims in his book Speed of Trust that the amount of trust, the speed at which things happen and costs go hand in hand. If there is little trust, then things happen slowly and costs rise. On the other hand, if there is more trust, then things happen faster and costs fall. My contact with the administrator points in the same direction. Work slows down and costs increase when my ability to assess the safety and necessity of the programs being downloaded onto my computer is not trusted. Half an hour of two people's working time costs money. The administrator will bill the company, and my time has a cost too. In addition, the opportunity cost of losing half an hour of work can easily be calculated by dividing my annual overall salary by work hours.

The example of MP shows how cautiousness can add costs in many different ways. The working time used by management, the amount of time it takes to make a decision, and good employees becoming frustrated costs money. It is extremely expensive when an employee decides to leave: it costs one and a half times an emp-loyee's annual salary.[223] The biggest costs may turn out to be factors affecting motivation, work efficiency, and the quality of cooperation. Unnecessary interruptions reduce time available for focused working, and changes to motivation reduce productivity.

---

222 I am unsure why Stephen named his son Stephen, but a name can turn out to be surprisingly valuable, for example when people Google the father and find the son. I may soon change my name to Steve H. Jobs.

223 Buckingham, M., Coffman, C., First, Break all the Rules: What the World's Greatest Managers Do Differently, 1999.

All this aggression and lack of motivation are pushed on us for the sole reason that rational fear has assumed an unreasonably large role in a company decision making. By reducing fear and adding trust, companies become leaner and smarter. Even where relations of power in a company and the roles of employees have been precisely defined, there is always room for personal decision making. Even in these situations, people make surprising decisions due to fear.

9.

We might have the wrong breed of idiots in corporations. My friend Marko Kulmala made me think about this, when he half jokingly threw an idea at me. He was playing around with the thought of offering companies a service called "Idiot." You could call in the idiot to help with a work meeting. The idiot would then behave like a four-year-old child, always asking questions when he or she did not understand. The idiot, being an idiot, would not be looking after his or her reputation or position in the group, given that an idiot's reputation is not likely to change, and that he or she would not need the approval of the group. This idea is brilliant in its simplicity. An outsider has the benefit of being the idiot. An outsider can ask questions that people who belong to the group are likely not to. The idiot can question the conventional wisdom of the company, the terms used, the plans made and whether the grounds they are based on are correct.

It often seems that people who at first seem to be of one mind in fact disagree violently. They have merely decided to remain silent and nod along in order to keep the peace. During meetings, people use terms that they do not understand. Or do understand, but in a different way than everyone present, even though they all use that term on a daily basis. Sometimes no one understands anything, but work is still carried out at full pace.

I was once witness to a conversation that could have been avoided had there been an idiot present. A room full of engineers in leading positions had gathered together to solve various serious challenges for the future of their work. Every engineer sitting in that room had a firm grasp of the technology, some had great skill at mathematics and a few had several patents to their name. Moreover, every one of them was extremely proud about their own expertise. As the discussion went on, the term "system" was thrown around – a key term for their work. Even though this was supposed to be a harmless term, it was followed by a passionate debate, where each in his turn amended or specified the previous speaker's definition of "system." In the end, after a heated and prolonged debate, one of the engineers asked to speak, and said: "I think it's no wonder we have problems if we all disagree on what 'system' means." The room fell quiet.

This resolved a lot of problems. After this moment of honesty and exposure, the group managed to ferret out a number of other ambiguous terms, the meaning of which no one had dared ask about, because they all assumed that the other members of the group knew the exact meaning of these terms. The members of the group felt that showing their own ignorance would have been extremely dangerous. Asking "stupid" questions is always a social risk, no matter what people claim. Among experts, one takes a huge risk by revealing that one does not know something.

Fear of losing social standing is a fairly reasonable fear. If a person's position or esteem falls in the eyes of others, it may have an effect on how colleagues treat him or her on an everyday basis. Calling the idiot to your meeting can clear the air and encourage group members to speak directly, honestly and without fear of being found out. However, in my experience the underlying fears connected to social standing only start going away once a group learns to engage in dialogue, which means a discussion where people try to reach shared terms and understand on a deeper level what the other person means. This kind of discussion creates a basis for deepening the trust between group members. When trust has a firm foundation, it can stand almost any kind of debate. A debate without trust easily devolves into warfare or social games. When there is a sense of trust, you can have even a vigorous exchange of opinions, which can lead to taking a group's thinking to another level. Trust, or what Stephen Porges calls "the neuroception of safety" is only created when enough group members expose themselves to ridicule, criticism, and loss of status, and manage to survive unscathed.

Follow the Leader

1.

In September 1924, the Neva River, which pierced what was then Soviet Leningrad, flowed onto the streets of the city. Even though floods due to the flow of water from the Bay of Finland were common in the city, this time the water rose to record heights. The surface of the river rose by 380 centimetres, and the streets of the city were full of flotsam brought in by the water. As the citizens fought against the rising water, there was full panic in one of the laboratories in Leningrad. The dogs, which had been locked into their cages, looked on helplessly as the water flowing into the kennels covered the floor, and kept rising. The water in the cages was churned into froth, as terrified dogs swam in place in order to keep their nostrils above the water so they could breathe.

The dogs, which were fighting for their lives, belonged to Soviet scientist Ivan Pavlov, who had earlier discovered conditioning, a key mechanism in learning. Even though the events that caused the flood had nothing to do with Pavlov, they did not become a simple nasty footnote in the history of the laboratory. Quite the opposite.

The animals were saved by a research assistant who let them out at the last moment. The remnants of the flood were cleaned up, Leningrad went on with its life and research in the laboratory continued. However, something had changed. The dogs, which had been conditioned to salivate when a bell was rung, no longer did so. The conditioning appeared to be gone. Pavlov had an idea. The fear experienced by the dogs appeared to have wiped away their programming. Or to be more precise: the dogs' fear had brainwashed them.[224]

Pavlov was a conscientious scientist. It was not enough for him that the programming had disappeared once – he wanted to repeat the experiment. The dogs were put in their cages, and Pavlov released water into the cages. Then they were released and tested. The conditioning was gone. As time went by, the research group once again conditioned the animals, put them in cages, and sprayed them with water until they panicked. Once again, the conditioning disappeared.

Lenin had granted Pavlov considerable recognition before,[225] but now, after Lenin's death, the Nobel Prize winning scientist had struck gold. His finding would have an effect that he himself would quite probably have disliked, as would those who dared to disagree with the official dogma emanating from the Kremlin. Pavlov had proved the crushing power of fear.

Even though Pavlov never quite toed the party line of the Soviet Union's leaders (neither Lenin nor his successors), his findings were used to effectively crush the opponents of the Party regime. Fear was a key tool in crushing people's wills, and the people in power were particularly enlightened when it came

---

224 The first one to write about this was William Sargant in Battle for the Mind, 1956. Dominic Streatfeild has also written about it in Brainwash, mainly based on Sargant's book. Details relating to the Neva floods have been taken from various sources, including: http://www.saint-petersburg.com/history/floods.asp

225 Lenin had invited Pavlov to the Kremlin a little while after the revolution, asking him to write everything he knew about conditioning animals. However, Lenin did tell Pavlov that he was not interested in animals per se, but rather in how Pavlov's theories and methods would affect people.

to using fear. Nevertheless, we should not think that fear only changes people in extreme conditions. It would also be a mistake to believe that fear is not used for conditioning or changing people on a regular basis.

2.

"Goddamnit!" The boss opens the sliding doors and steps into the room. "Shit, fuck, bugger!" The open plan office, located in Helsinki, falls silent. Everyone keeps their eyes fixed firmly on their screens, as they know that in the best case scenario the whole team will get a bollocking. However, with bad luck an individual team member will get the special treatment from the boss, and that is not a risk that anyone wants to take. For that reason, they also avoid eye contact. However, the day's scapegoat has already been picked. The boss goes to him and lets him have it. The diatribe is a mix of business and personal. This situation is hardly unique, as there is always something to get upset about. They never know what, but just from the gleam in the boss's eyes, they know that it is about to happen.

Finally, the boss turns around, closes the sliding doors behind him, and allows silence to fall over the room. Leila and the other members of the team know that there will be another discussion over phones that evening. They have made a habit of venting their feelings about what happened during the day. It makes people feel better, and makes the boss's behaviour easier to understand, and in the end people manage to deal with it. These conversations make those days just a little more bearable, when the reasons for the boss's tantrums do not feel logical or fair. Generally, the only thing they are able to discern is how much he hates and disdains his employees, but sometimes Leila and the other staff are able to grasp what may have been behind a given outburst.[226]

The boss usually closets himself in his room after an outburst. Leila has also been the brunt of his abuse on several occasions. He usually makes up for his fits for example by taking an individual or the whole team out to lunch: "Let's go downstairs together. I'm buying." This is also something that everyone in the team has gotten used to. The matter itself is never discussed, and he never apologises. He makes up for his behaviour with a friendly comment or lunch. And, because they cannot change their boss, they just need to get everything out of the good moments. Generally, the next outburst does not begin during the make up lunch.

The boss is very good at breaking up the solidarity of the employees. One day, Leila is working along at the office, where 6 people would normally be working, when the sliding doors to the boss's office open. However, this time there is no abuse but rather a task for Leila. He asks her to write a letter of termination for her colleague. Leila objects. She is neither a supervisor nor does she want to participate in firing her colleague. Leila tries to persuade her boss to say it to her colleague's face, but entreaties and objections have no effect. The boss makes her write the letter and put it on the desk of her colleague. He takes off, and Leila feels it is her duty to wait for her colleague to arrive. After he comes back, opens the letter and reads its contents, Leila looks at him and admits that she has written the letter: "He forced me to write it."

---

226 Based on an interview with "Leila" on 5 February 2013.

Even though connecting leadership through fear with brainwashing may be problematic, methods of brainwashing and their effects have a marked similarity to this kind of leadership. It is in a twisted way like domestic abuse, where violent acts are followed by making up. Alternatively, it is the working life version of Stockholm Syndrome, where employees become attached to their abuser.

There is a particularly disturbing link between a boss who leads through fear and interview methods aimed at controlling people. Constantly swinging from one emotional extreme to the other resembles a brainwashing technique where the interview is at one moment kind, and cruel the next. The essential thing about this alternation between friendly and cruel is that the target has no way of predicting what will come next. This behaviour is not based on logic or cause of effect; anything can happen at any time. Taken to its extreme, the interviewer changes his behaviour so often and so suddenly that in the end the only point of reference for the interviewee is the interviewer. It is a common theme in brainwashing methods to isolate a person from her group, and to control her speech, behaviour and even bodily functions.

Brainwashing takes place in controlled environments, and a work community is therefore not the best place for full on brainwashing. However, we should think about when leading stops being mostly about accomplishing something and turns into maximising the leader's position of power. Where lies the border between healthy, and unhealthy use of power?

We seem to have a kind of instinctive need for approval from people in positions of power. For some reason, praise from a quirky and fear-mongering boss means more to us than a thank you from a harmless or friendly supervisor. Even in this work community there were good times when the employees were thanked for successfully doing their jobs. Interestingly, Leila still seems anxious when she tells about the acts of terror directed against her self-esteem and the whole work community. However, when she tells about the grateful and laudatory feedback given by her boss, her posture improves and her gaze grows bright.

As the relations of power become simpler, something else happens. Through his mood shifts and extreme reactions, the boss keeps the employees constantly on their toes, with all the power in his hands. At the same time, he forces his employees to stay in their roles, where they are unable to express their abilities. There is one dictator in the company, and the rest are peons.

Antonio Cazorla Sánchez' *Fear and Progress*,[227] which deals with the period of Spanish dictator Francisco Franco's reign from the perspective of ordinary people, is a good portrayal of this kind of setting. In this dictatorship, which revolved around Franco, the only task the poor, common folk had was to obey orders. Obedience was more important than understanding Franco's principles – not that anyone really did understand them. Even though the people obeyed their ruler, a survey in 1950 among army recruits shows that only 5% of recruits understood even the rudiments of Franco's political principles.

Leading through fear does exactly the same in companies as Franco's political model did in Spain and Pavlov's observations in the hands of Soviet leaders. It is used as a tool to prop up leaders and to break resistance. One person thinks, others do, and gradually the dissidents are broken.

---

227 Cazorla Sánchez, A., *Fear and Progress: Ordinary Lives in Franco's Spain, 1939–1975*, 2010.

3.

Leila provides an apt description of how the behaviour of a person leading through fear changes people. Her as well. Leila proposed less initiatives of her own, and her thinking changed. When she was leading a project, she no longer thought about what would be the best option for the project, but rather what the boss might prefer. When she came up with ideas of her own, she kept them to herself. "Won't work" was her boss's standard answer, one that never needed justification. Her boss, on the other hand, had plenty of ideas. Leila describes him as one of the most imaginative and dynamic people she has ever met. However, some of his ideas were, in the view of the team, impractical, while others were outright absurd and offensive.

One of her boss's ideas has stuck with Leila: a chauvinistic newspaper advert that Leila objected to. Her objection was however of no use, and the notice was printed. The target group of the advertisement provided a huge amount of negative feedback. The boss was unmoved. His next idea was already on the table, and the team did not want to start a war by dwelling on the previous one. The team never dared to confront their boss about his behaviour. Due to his mood changes, he was too dangerous.

In the end, her boss's behaviour made Leila think about why she was working for a company managed in such a mentally destructive way. Leila's boss tried to deflect her desire to leave the company with a pay raise. She originally wanted to get her boss to terminate her, but in the end she notified him that she was resigning.

Leila's last day was typical, with its ups and downs. Leila's boss told her that he would come by in the afternoon to say goodbye. Leila got her hopes up; perhaps her boss would say a few words in parting and thank her for a job well done. The afternoon dragged by, with no boss in sight. Finally, after three o'clock, he sent a message: "Not coming. You can go."

It has been a few years since these events by the time I meet Leila. She is a thirty-something, well-educated woman who is successful at her present job. She gives a confident impression. Leila looks me straight in the eyes without coming off as intimidating. She sits straight and is dressed in a youthful beige suit. Looking at her, it is difficult to believe that she has at some time turned her gaze down in the face of an arbitrary boss. However, that was an everyday event in a company where the employees were dominated by a terrorising boss.

Systematically (intentionally or unintentionally) undermining a person's self-esteem and position is something that is difficult to stop and difficult to resist. The key thing is that it happens gradually. Just like with domestic abuse, the victims are often unable to make a distinction between normal and unhealthy behaviour. One can only understand the mechanisms of undermining and their effect if one sees them happen to a loved one or to oneself. When someone with whom you are constantly involved with makes you feel uncertain, it tends to grow. In the end, Leila started to doubt herself: "My own opinion of myself started to sink. I was badly stuck. I couldn't get out. I was a shadow of myself. I realised that I had to get out. Or there would have been little left of me." Leila was only able to make a precise analysis of events at her next job. She regained her initiative and started to do well. It was only when the evidence piled up that she started to change her view of herself: "It turned out that I'm not the kind of person that I was told."[228]

4.

One of the things that seems to encourage fear-based leadership is our love for mythical leaders. The directors of successful companies often wind up on the covers and in the editorials of magazines and as the subjects of biographies, as their principles are squeezed into simple models. Of course, there is nothing wrong with that. Learning from a model is effective, and a message usually sinks in better if it is simple. We should not underestimate the abilities of these successful leaders, but focusing on one person still gives a distorted picture of how companies succeed. Of course, a leader has an enormous effect on the operations and culture of a company, but sometimes, along with the big story about a super leader's larger than life thoughts, there is another, far less noticeable story of what the qualities of a successful leader are. One good example is Steve Jobs, who is the archetype of a modern leader. But we have to ask, in what direction is this archetype pushing the many leaders who want to be just like him?

---

228 Leila visibly lit up when asked about her current bosses, who listen to and value her opinions. The end results of projects are discussed in advance, but she can carry out her work independently, with supervisors trusting Leila to know what to do. Rather than having to constantly ask her bosses about things, she is allowed to use her own judgment and experience when making decisions. Mistakes do not result in public humiliation, but are rather a learning experience. Furthermore, at her new job, the boss is willing to admit he has made mistakes, like anyone else.

Jobs, founder of Apple, died on 5 October 2011.[229] The company was in great shape, and Jobs' reputation as a business genius was at its apex. The iPhone had disrupted the smartphone market, iTunes had revolutionised music and movie distribution, and the iPad, published about a year earlier, was quickly changing the concept of mobile computers, and was set to disrupt the business of magazine and book publishing. Jobs' appearances at Apple product releases had been like rock concerts, but also led to disrupting sector after sector. The Apple Company[230] broke all previous records both in terms of profit figures and stock prices. The myth of Jobs was propped up on a solid foundation. He quickly became the archetype of a visionary leader: a model for future leaders, a leader who could sniff out the future decades in advance and could form R&D and market research teams on his own, a leader who made quick and hard decisions and crushed all obstacles in his way. Jobs' incredible success seems to show that his way of leading was unbeatable.

Walter Isaacson's biography portrays a leader who led through vision and fear. Jobs was omnipotent, defining the laws of the universe and either opening the gates to heaven for his underlings – or condemned them to Hell. Based on statements from various sources, one finds a way of leadership that is masculine in the extreme. One alpha male leads a pack which is in the grips of a struggle both inside and between packs. The recipe for success is to focus on the individual, which was certainly the case for Apple. One person, one idea, one way of doing things.

---

229 Despite his magical abilities as an influencer, even Jobs was unable to avoid his fate. The limits of his reality distortion field were met.

230 Which is what Forrest Gump called Apple Computer Inc.

In this kind of culture, it is easy to recognise the protagonists and antagonists, i.e., the goodies and the baddies. In the precautionary stories told in companies, the successes and failures of individuals are often brought up. Everyone who works in a group knows who is part of a higher case, and who a lower caste. It was in fact typical for Jobs to think that people were either enlightened, or shitheads. There was no middle ground. The "Gods" were raised on a pedestal, while at the same time every one of them knew that they were in no way different from the engineers Jobs had tagged as shitheads. The "Gods" were constantly afraid that the truth would be revealed, and they would be exiled from paradise. It was not always nice to be in the same room with Jobs.

This same judgment day mood could be found elsewhere as well. There was a persistent rumour at Apple, according to which Jobs might start a discussion with anyone he met at the company, and would fire them on the spot if he did not understand what the stammering, frightened person in front of him was doing in the company. These express firings even had a name: "Got Steved."[231] It is quite likely that no one ever really got fired like this, but it was enough that people believed such a thing was possible. Employees froze up when Jobs was around.

According to Steve Wozniak, the co-founder of Apple, "Steve could have accomplished what he did without the many stories about how he terrorised his own people." The Jobs biography by Walter Isaacson seems to also put forward the view that Jobs' impulsive and offensive behaviour would not have been necessary

---

231 Leander Kahney, among others, has written about this fast lane firing in *Inside Steve's Brain*, 2008.

in order to reach Apple's astonishing results. For example, the Macintosh was late on schedule and expenses were greater than predicted precisely due to Jobs' violent interventions.[232] Some of those who worked with Jobs feel that Isaacson's biography is a little too bleak. One of them is marketer Ken Segall, who worked with Jobs at Apple and Next for over a decade. In his view, Isaacson's book is accurate, but the tone is too negative. Segall felt that it was easy to work with Jobs if you were good at what you did. However, Segall has admitted that when he stopped working at Apple, he felt a great sensation of relief knowing that Jobs would no longer call him at all hours in order to comment on something or to make demands.[233] During 12 years, Segall only got a proper shouting on 2 occasions.

We should take a closer look at the myth of Jobs. Iconic leaders have a great effect on what people think is good or bad in a style of leadership. Even though people often try to model leadership and dress it up as a science, it is anything but.[234] It is more of an art, which can however benefit from scientific resources. An archetype of a mythical leader is painted onto leaders and managers by stories told by consultants, coaches, books and the media. The struggle between ideals decides which archetype they adopt when

---

232 Even though provoking fear in others is a form of manipulation in itself, Jobs had other means as well. One of these methods was known inside the company as the "reality distortion field." A person who had a strong opinion when going in to see Jobs would find themselves thinking quite differently – in agreement with Jobs – at the end of the meeting. This also had its benefits. When a person is manipulated into believing in the impossible, he or she often turns out to be capable of it.

233 Ken Segall talked about his experiences of Jobs at a Business Summit event in Helsinki on 3 June 2014, organised by the Nordic Business Forum.

234 No model or survey will ever capture the complex world in which decision makers operate on a daily basis. Success can be achieved in many different ways. Furthermore, modelling tends to discount the role of sheer dumb luck.

approaching their employees. It is therefore far from irrelevant what kind of archetype leaders admire and imitate.

Who knows – perhaps Jobs' management philosophy is superb. However, the important thing is not whether it can deliver results, but rather at what cost. One could on good grounds claim that Jobs' style of leading, centred on his own persona, was certainly not the most humane way of reaching results. One could equally claim that the model of an organisational Jesus is not the only way to reach exceptional results – there are also ways of doing this that do not involve mental abuse or fear.

5.

In 2004, Jenn Lim was tasked with compiling a fascinating and dangerous corporate manual. In fact, it was not exactly a business manual project, but rather a risky attempt to collect the uncensored thoughts of Zappos employees about the culture of Zappos. This was the birth of the culture book of online store Zappos. Jenn Lim was tasked with compiling the book. At first, she thought it was a risky project. They were about to give people the chance to speak their minds, along with the promise to publish everything they said. It seemed like a crazy idea – no one had done anything like it before. They had no experience of whether such a method would work, and whether the end result would actually resemble the Zappos culture. It seemed equally frightening to think that the book might reveal the things that were not perfect about the company, and of course whether the employees thought that Zappos was as good a place to work as the management thought Zappos is not a conventional company, and the Zappos culture book is not a conventional book. Zappos was founded in the late 1990s, when Tony Hsieh got the spark to establish an online store specialising in footwear. The idea seemed daft at first, but after juggling the numbers for a while, Hsieh became convinced that people bought a lot of shoes on the net. A lot.

The money for the company came from the Venture Frogs, a capital investment company owned by Tony and his fellow owners of the Link Exchange company, which had been sold for a large sum of money. At first, Zappos grew at a breathtaking pace, but it proved hard to turn a profit. Gradually, the company ate up both the investment firm's funds and Tony Hsieh's personal resources. The bursting of the internet bubble scared off external investors, leaving the company to fend for itself. Loss of liquidity forced Hsieh to cut wages, lay off staff, offer lodgings to some employees on company premises (which were a large flat), cut the marketing budget, and serve customers in such a way that they started to market Zappos to each other. Management and employees made financial and professional compromises, and as a result, the Zappos culture developed as a by-product of the chaotic atmosphere in which the company operated at the time. Of course, at the time the management did not know whether there was anything special about the Zappos culture, or whether that was just the view from within.

The famous Zappos culture book was born when a group of Zappos staff were discussing in a bar how Zappos could recruit only the best people who optimally suited the culture of the company. There was one recently hired employee present, so Tony asked everyone there to tell their own version of what they saw as the Zappos culture. After the round was over, Tony realised that something special had happened in that room. They had just described more or less perfectly what the Zappos culture was about. This set in motion the Zappos culture book. Tony decided to ask all employees what the Zappos culture meant for them, and to publish their answers in a book.

There was no plan B – which is in itself rather typical of Zappos. Their method is to try, and if the attempt fails, to learn from it. According to Lim, Zappos wanted every employee to give their frank opinion. Good or bad, it did not matter so long as every comment was open and came straight from the heart.[235]

In autumn 2004, Zappos employees received an email from Tony, asking them for 100-500 word texts about what the Zappos culture meant to them. "The culture of our company is a combination of what our employees think our culture is, so we wanted to collect all of these thoughts in the book." The first culture book was published according to this original plan. The texts were not vetted, amended or censored. The only editing they did was to correct typos.

There is something frightening about this method – not for employees, but for the managment. When the texts are published unedited, except for typos, what ends up in the book is the truth. All flaws are revealed. By reading the book, you can dig into the guts of the company's culture, and the mood of the company, which are otherwise so hard to grasp. These days, the Zappos culture book is an annually published, 300 page collection of

---

235 I talked with Jenn Lim in person in Helsinki on 9 September 2013 and via Skype on 3 October 2013. In addition, I met with Jamie Naughton, a member of Zappos' management, on 21 May 2014. We discussed corporate culture, and furthermore Jamie talked about Zappos at the Jobs for the Future seminar organised in Helsinki on 22 May 2014. I have also used Tony Hsieh's *Delivering Happiness* as a source, a book that is co-authored by Jenn Lim.

stories, remarks and opinions and still represents the views of every member of the company's staff. Contributing is voluntary, and employees can choose whether to have texts printed under their own name or anonymously. Most choose the former.

The best or the worst thing about the book is that anyone can access it, including me. The book is just a mouse click away on Amazon. For a reader used to ordinary corporate culture, it makes for a jarring experience. For example, Zappos is often described as a family. There are plenty of individual examples of how colleagues have helped each other move house, how family members have been drawn in, and how employees have supported each other during times of bereavement. Many texts dwell on how important laughter is at Zappos; the figures range from one to seven good laughs a day. The term "awesome" tends to pop up. The staff have even come up with a name for themselves: the Zapponians.

Reading the texts, I am amazed by how often the company's values are mentioned. Through my work, I have read and heard thousands of people describe their companies, and I have never heard of such an extensive and deep adoption of company values. Of course, adoption is not really the right word. In fact, company employees have captured the company's values for themselves. For the Zapponians, the company's values are not buzzwords, but rather something that they see realised in their daily lives.

Moreover, perhaps the most touching thing about the book is how sincerely surprised and grateful the employees are about being allowed to, or more correctly being encouraged to be themselves at their workplace. One writer was thankful of being accepted as she was – a blue haired geek. Another contributor told about how the Zappos culture had changed his relationship with work, and made him more creative, adventurous, loving and generous while working at the company.

It is hard to even imagine a better way of dispersing the fears established in work communities than to encourage people to think that they are fine just as they are, and that the rough edges are actually advantages. The culture book is a message about who has the right to speak, and how. Every person at Zappos has that right, a right which is furthermore unlimited. In addition to the culture book, there is in general an open conversational culture at the company. Some people may be surprised that a message sent to the CEO will be answered during the same day, in person. Not exactly common in a big company. Tony also has an "Ask Tony" column where people can ask him anything about the company and its operations.

Let me provide a good, recent example of Zappos practices. An employee sent Tony a question about her own supervisor. She named the supervisor and asked Tony what to do, as she felt the supervisor was not acting in accordance with company values. Hsieh decided to publish the question. It was a hard decision, but one based on his promise to company staff that all decisions relating to the company's culture would be transparent. Nothing would be swept under the carpet.

During the last few years, Zappos has consistently been listed as one of the top 40 companies to work at in the US, reaching at best sixth place. This is an incredible achievement. Of course, Zappos is not perfect, and people have their gripes. However, the practice of revealing these gripes for all keeps the fear in check. Dissident opinions are not punished, and the company's communications staff do not censor opinions that do not fit with the mainstream. Amidst the gushing praise, company personnel feel confident in expressing their own views, and furthermore that these views will be listened to. Some personnel object to the company's moving to the centre of Las Vegas, while others feel there is too much company politics, while still others have not fully adopted the Zappos culture. Some feel that the Zappos culture is declining. This is something that Jenn Lim noticed years ago. Gradually, a cross current has been created between old and new employees. Older employees sometimes feel frustrated with how little new staff understand about the company's history and about how the Zappos culture came to be what it is.[236] There are also those who feel that things were better before.

According to Jenn Lim, there have been few negative comments in the book over the years, and still fewer of these have been anonymous. She feels that the Zappos culture book helps people get along, particularly when it comes to the relationships between different employee roles. The fact that the company encourages staff to share their opinions and to tell supervisors what they think is a strong message from company management. Moreover, Lim feels that it is not just what employees say, but what the company does about disclosed problems that matters. When working with other companies, Lim often hears employee complaints about how the management asks staff what they think, but never does anything with this information. Employees

---

236 A typical excerpt concerning the subject: "When I think of the Zappos Culture I think of how great it all sounds and how great it all used to be. But lately they have been falling short of following through with all the promises. A lot of departments seem to have time to participate in all the activities, but other departments are so busy that they aren't given the time to participate." (excerpt from Zappos culture book).

quickly grow resigned, and an air of indifference sets in. Why bother, when management clearly does not.

The question is, does an emphasis on culture and employee happiness actually affect a company's bottom line, bringing dough and value to shareholders? In less than a decade, Zappos reached a billion dollars in revenue. In 2009, the company was sold to Amazon for 1.2 billion dollars. The company is turning a profit and is still growing.[237] As one text in the culture book put it: "Zappos has restored my faith in the teachings of my parents, teachers and customers. People can be nice, worthy of trust, respect the privacy of others, promote co-operation and still manage to be extremely successful at business."

The company's values provide another clue as to how to turn a profit. Their first value is to create "wow experiences" for customers through their services. At the same time, they emphasise creating a family like atmosphere, humility, doing more with less, reaching for personal growth and development, having fun, and sometimes doing the unexpected. All of this shows. When people are not afraid or anxious, they become socially open, enter a creative mindset, and have enough energy for both customers and work duties. As I stated before, Zappos is not a perfect company, nor am I trying to portray it as such. However, it is a good example of how to succeed in a humane way. An atmosphere without fear can turn vicious competition into play, and encourage employees

---

237 The company is now part of Amazon, so they do not give their figures to outsiders. This information is from Jamie Naughton of Zappos, according to whom Zappos has long ago exceeded the 1.5 billion dollar turnover it had at the moment of sale.

to get creative and to learn new things.[238] Happy (i.e., fearless) people get sick less, have less sick days, are more creative in everyday service situations and pass positive feelings on to customers.

6.

Every leader wants to get results. The books and articles written about leaders, as well as the stories and myths told about them usually promise to reveal the behaviour and assumptions that laid the ground for their success. The problem is, results can be achieved through very different methods. Moreover, achieving results does not equal being a good leader.[239] One must also consider the cost at which the results have been achieved, and what lies behind the leader's actions.

The myth of Steve Jobs represents one leadership archetype, while Tony Hsieh and his colleagues at Zappos are at the other end of the scale. In fact, Hsieh is the complete opposite of a controlling and omniscient alpha leader. He is usually described as an introvert, who believes that happy people are the best

---

238 Jenn Lim often sees fear at workplaces. The greatest fear right now is fear of losing one's job. In his experience, people are afraid that they will be punished by their boss for stating their honest opinion. In some companies, people are afraid that they are not liked. According to Lim, a culture book like the one by Zappos can help reduce these fears, though the same can be achieved using a different, alternative method that shows people that the organisation is encouraging them to communicate freely. Delivering Happiness, a company founded by Lim and Tony Hsieh, carries out change projects in companies that want to adopt happiness as their business model

239 For you shareholders: shareholder value is a flat and one dimensional metric for company value.

foundation for a company's culture.[240] If one were to look for what Hsieh and Jobs have in common, it would be an intense interest in customer experiences, and of course exceptional business sense.[241] That is just about all they have in common; they are as different as leaders possibly can be. Zappos' myth is underpinned by more or less democratic principles, according to which everyone has a right to make important decisions relating to customer experiences – not just company management. The only failure is never to try. Hsieh seems to be guided by the idea that, besides financial results, a company should produce good things for its employees and customers. For example, by "delivering happiness to people."[242]

One can further develop the difference between these two types of leaders by relying on the archetype theory of Robert Moore and Douglas Gillette.[243] In 1990, Moore and Gillette published King, Warrior, Magician and Lover. Even though the title sounds like a historical novel, it is in fact an exploration of Jungian archetype psychology by Moore, a psychologist, and Gillette, a mystic. Over twenty years ago, these writers were talking about a crisis of manhood, and in particular how manhood is misinterpreted. The greatest distortion is patriarchal

---

240 I have heard this same description from all those who have met Tony Hsieh or worked with him.

241 Though Hsieh seems to explain his success through sheer random chance.

242 Tony Hsieh wrote *Delivering Happiness* about the founding of Zappos.

243 Archetypes are part of Jungian psychology. Even though Jungians may disagree, the existence of these archetypes has never been proven. Obtaining such proof may be empirically impossible, or the archetypes might not even exist. However, archetypes can be useful, as in the present case. They provide a model and a language through which we can discuss an observation or phenomenon, or possibly through which we can lose ourselves and others in superficially deep sounding symbology. I try to avoid the latter.

culture, which is mistakenly seen as manly culture. Moore and Gillette claim that this is in fact boyish culture, a psychologically immature expression of masculinity that is based on fear. Only an immature man insecure in his masculinity is afraid of women and fully psychologically developed men.

Historically, leading has been men's work. Fortunately, this situation is being remedied by small, but positive steps. Men have for so long determined how power is to be used and how leadership is to be defined that it is worth looking at the roots of these practices,[244] as they have an effect on how people are treated and evaluated in today's workplaces.

Moore and Gillette have noticed that men stuck at the boy stage of psychology rise to leadership positions and refuse to accept more developed behaviour among their employees, especially among women. Full femininity and masculinity is frightening. This is expressed in how the boss lets out his fear in the form of envy and attacks those who are more skilled than himself. This behaviour can manifest as either open attacks or passive aggressiveness.

Moore and Gillette's work, carried out over two decades ago, divides the male psyche into four archetypes: king, magician, warrior and lover. According to them, a man has grown to his full psychological potential only after achieving all these archetypes. As a man develops, all these archetypes have a positive effect on his behaviour. In practice, he leads in a wise and egalitarian

---

244 Personally, I see no reason why Moore's and Gillette's archetype theory could not be applied to women, by for example substituting the queen for the king, or a gender neutral word like ruler. However, Moore and Gillette talk about men, and I do not want to put words in their mouths or to extend their theory beyond what they intended.

manner. A leader is thus able to use his full mental capacity and creativity in his work, to act without fear, and to accept his own instincts. But – always but – it is not quite that simple, as each archetype also has its shadows. If one is not fully mature, then the active or passive shadow becomes dominant.

This kind of symbolism might mean a great deal to people, but I am rather sceptical about whether such a system of archetypes really exists. On the other hand this does not make Moore and Gillette's ideas worthless. In this context, archetypes give us a way of looking at what kind of leadership is good and what is bad. Each shadow has its active and passive sides. The active shadow of the king is a tyrant, and the passive shadow is a weakling. Both lead to fear at the workplace.

The tyrant drains the oxygen out of a work community and drives people to the edge of a breakdown. According to Moore and Gillette, a leader regresses into a tyrant due to fear. He is afraid of losing his position, and turns that fear into anger. When a tyrant king is not in the spotlight, he turns destructive, merciless and ruthless. He is terrified about his own weakness and is afraid of being found out. The tyrant king is sensitive to criticism and feels weak and powerless at even the smallest setback or comment. His personality is underpinned by feelings of worthlessness, vulnerability and weakness. Often, the people under him do not notice this – all they see is the rage. The king's passive shadow, i.e., the weakling, spreads uncertainty through his behaviour.

The magician works in the world of ideas, and is able to turn thoughts into acts and things. Doctors, engineers, innovators, teachers and other experts are typical magicians. The active shadow of the magician is the manipulator. The manipulator manipulates others for personal gain, stifles their growth and jealously guards his knowledge. The passive shadow is an irresponsible "innocent," a person who wants all the glory, but takes no responsibility for his actions, and may even be unaware of their consequences.

The warrior archetype portrays how good a person is at working with his own feelings and the feelings of others. The active shadow of the warrior is a sadist, and the passive one a masochist.

The fourth and last archetype is the lover. His active shadow makes the person addicted to satisfying his urges, and the passive shadow makes a person unable to love.

It is important to note that these are not people, but myths and images attributed to "superstar leaders." They have an effect on what kind of leadership the people climbing the corporate ladder think is good or bad leadership. The archetype attributable to the myth of Jobs seems to be a combination of two active shadow archetypes, those of the king and the magician. The mythical Apple founder is a manipulative tyrant, who with his "reality distortion fields" uses every manipulative tool in his arsenal, and who also possesses sadistic qualities.[245]

---

245 One could make a game of analysing the leadership styles of historical leaders or one's own bosses, by comparing them to different archetypes or shadows. You can start with Hitler and move on to your own boss. (Spoiler: Hitler is a tyrant, manipulator, sadist and addict. Strongly active shadow.)

In *Delivering Happiness*,[246] Tony Hsieh describes Zappos' early years with a quotation from Alexandre Dumas' musketeers: "One for all and all for one!" This brotherly vision cannot be realised if leaders behave towards their employees like Moore and Gillette's shadows. A work community can also succeed when, instead of focusing on individual egos and the rivalry between alpha figures, the alphas and betas work in mixed packs, with the understanding that no one is to be snapped at or eaten. This "musketeer" model has at least three major image problems: it seems like a soft hippie utopia, it is as yet (until very recently) unproven in big companies, and it is hard to write about. It is easier for the press to write about individual leaders than a company's culture, which is furthermore a very vague concept. However, during the last few years companies like Zappos have become big enough that people have had to at least question the conventional hero-leader models. These companies have shown that models based on something completely different than group hierarchy, fear and individual superstars can work in firms with a turnover of over a billion dollars, not just in small, creative enterprises.[247]

Leadership using the model of a mature leader is considerably harder and takes more work than leading through fear. Of course, it has its problems as well. As one contributor to Zappos'

---

246 Hsieh, T., Delivering Happiness, 2010.

247 Going back to what Jack Welch of GE has said about corporate culture, transfer of power, making things simple and communication, it seems like he has much in common with the ideas underpinning Zappos. Despite his reputation as a trouble-shooter, Welch was very much interested in people.

culture book put it: "Who is actually in charge of this place?" However, the question is which of these models would people rather see at their workplace, and which of them will in the end prove sustainable.

How to Lead Hairless Apes

1.

"Real power is based on fear." This comment was made by a manager who worked with me on the same project. "Just like in the *Life of Pi*."

In *Life of Pi*, written by Yann Martel, protagonist Piscine Molitor Patel, AKA Pi, is marooned in a lifeboat with a fully grown Bengalese tiger. Pi has spent his whole life learning how to handle animals. For example, he knows that "The animal in front of you must know where it stands, whether above you or below you. Social rank is central to how it leads its life. Rank determines whom it can associate with and how; where and when it can eat; where it can rest; where it can drink; and so on. Until it knows its rank for certain, the animal lives a life of unbearable anarchy. It remains nervous, jumpy, dangerous. Luckily for the circus trainer, decisions about social rank among higher animals are not always based on brute force. Hediger (1950) says, "When two creatures meet, the one that is able to intimidate its opponent is recognised as socially superior, so that a social decision does not always depend on a fight; an encounter in some circumstances may be enough."[248] A mutual, silent agreement about social hierarchy can momentarily defuse a situation, but fear can prove dangerous as a tool of power. Martel writes that an animal tamer must remain a super alpha, and slipping and becoming a beta carries a heavy price.

---

248 Martel, Y., Life of Pi, 2001.

You can achieve power through fear, but is it real power, and is it ultimately useful for anything else except temporarily bolstering the fear monger's own position?[249] There is always someone waiting for the fear monger's power to wane, ready to pounce when they have a weak moment. Dictators always get deposed, alphas have to submit or be killed. On the other hand, one could think that a power vacuum is no different – it can create chaos, and therefore fear.

This kind of thinking is based on the assumption that humans are pack animals, dependent on hierarchies. There is of course some basis in this, as humans have lived in packs throughout their evolutionary history. However, there is a fundamental misunderstanding here about how pack animals, particularly apes, operate in their natural environment.

2.

In March 2013, something extraordinary happened in the Lake Tanganyika area in Tanzania. An alpha chimpanzee called Pimu started a fight with the male chimpanzee that was second in the pack's pecking order. This second chimpanzee, which lost the fight, had to leave the pack. Normally, the pack would return to its normal routines and order within a day – but not this time. The morning after the pack alpha and second in command had their fight, four other males from the same pack attacked the

---

249 I cannot overemphasise here that hard decisions, clear choices and astute vision can be carried out and promoted through other feeling than fear. It is a question of whether one decides to use fear to lead, and particularly what the motive for such use would be.

alpha male, and beat and bit it to death. A male chimpanzee's greatest threat usually comes from outside, but there were no other chimpanzee packs in the area. With no external threats and the second in command exiled, the subordinate males in the pack saw that their time had come, and decided to get rid of their leader.

Pimu's fate is in line with the received wisdom about how pack animals behave and the law of nature. This is a world embroiled in a constant struggle for leadership and survival, a struggle where the strongest and most aggressive triumph. The pack can maintain order and peace only when the pack alpha is so frightening that the subordinate males do not dare challenge him for leadership. In addition to ruling itself through fear, the pack also needs an external threat in order to maintain internal hierarchy. These kinds of anecdotes may make use believe that this is exactly how the world, and nature work. Fear keeps communities in order, and violent behaviour is normal. This conclusion is often and easily smuggled into the human context, as man is after all nothing but a hairless ape. Therefore the same rules must apply to us.

However, drawing direct conclusions from stories like the above may turn out to be a serious mistake. Things are not always what they seem at first, not even in the animal world.

3.

In the early 1980s, biologist Robert Sapolsky had the opportunity to observe an extremely unusual chain of events. For several years, Sapolsky practically lived in a nature reserve in Kenya with a group of baboons that he dubbed the "Forest

Group." Forest Group members acted as one might expect. They spent their days carrying out everyday baboon chores, such as looking for food and grooming other pack members. Sapolsky frequently witnessed outbursts of aggression toward pack mates. The baboons would often attack females or lower ranking males. The constant threat of violence seemed to be part of the baboons' lives.

However, something took place in the neighbouring pack's territory that would change the lives of both packs forever. A nearby tourist village stepped up its operations, more tourists came in, and the village produced a gradually increasing amount of waste. Food scraps flowed into the dump: half eaten hamburgers, chocolate cakes, chicken legs and more. It was like a banquet was being set for the baboons, which are omnivorous. The pack living closest to the dump dug into this horn of plenty, and started to live the good life. Food was always available, and the males did not need to exert themselves in order to get their daily calories. Finally, the pack members were sleeping in trees with branches overhanging the dump. The overweight "Dump Group" baboons did not need to even walk to breakfast, as they would simply drop from their trees to poke at their own breakfast buffet in the form of fresh scraps brought to the dump.

The Forest Group also eventually found the food scraps. One day, half the males in the pack skipped the monthly routine of grooming other pack members, and instead of working on their social relationships decided to head to the dump to fight over the scraps. The Dump Group tried to stop the Forest Group baboons from getting to the food. However, despite scuffles, both packs got what they wanted – there were plenty of food scraps. However, the fates of both packs changed when the humans tipped spoiled meat into the dump. As per usual, the strongest males in the packs fought over the best titbits. However, these titbits turned out to be more than they bargained for, as they carried mycobacterium tuberculosis bacteria, better known as tuberculosis.

During the next year, tuberculosis wiped out almost the entire Dump Group. It also took out the Forest Group males who had gone raiding the dump. The disease wiped out the dump raiders, which is to say the most aggressive adult males in the pack, the ones who had had the strength to win the fight over the spoiled meat at the dump.

According to Sapolsky, the death of the most aggressive males had a crucial effect on social relationships in the pack. Not only were there suddenly less males in comparison to females, but the males were also less aggressive. The Forest Group still had a loose hierarchy, but the behaviour of high ranking males changed completely from what can be considered normal for baboon packs. High ranking males very rarely harassed other pack members, and sometimes even shared their food with them. Females and males groomed each others' fur more often, and Sapolsky even witnessed several occasions when males groomed each other. According to him, this practically never happens among baboons living in the wild.

Sapolsky has stated that the reduction of males in the pack had an effect, but it does not explain by itself why the pack's behaviour changed so radically. The more important factor was the selection of those that remained. Aggressive males had died due to tuberculosis from the meat, while the less aggressive, who had not had access to the meat, survived.

4.

Sapolsky last went to meet the Forest Group in 2009. He has not returned to the area since then, as the sad fact is that the group has practically ceased to exist. With increased human contact, the baboons gradually got used to people, and started getting more curious and aggressive towards humans. The baboons no longer operate as a group, but rather wander around as individuals. If they happen to cross one of the many invisible boundaries set by human beings, they are killed without mercy.

However, for a few decades the behaviour of the Forest Group was exceptional by baboon standards. The amount of aggression plummeted and pack members were intensely involved in many forms of social interaction. Even though all the original males who had been in the forest group when the tuberculosis deaths occurred had long since died, the pack still behaved in the same way.

Even though Sapolsky is uncertain about the reasons that these changes persisted, he does have one explanation. In baboon packs the females stay with the pack into which they are born, while the males leave to join other packs. Coming to a new pack is extremely stressful and dangerous for these young males. It is like the initiation rituals organised for young would be gang members. The other males will attack the newcomer. He will be constantly intimidated, with little hope of attention from the pack's females. In this case, newcomers to the pack were accepted in what is for baboons a friendly manner. The new males were not intimidated, and the females would groom new pack members approximately four times more frequently than in other packs. In addition, females were ready to have sexual intercourse with newcomers within, on average, 18 days from arrival, with actual coitus taking place, on average, on the twentieth day. For other packs, the corresponding figures are 63 and 78 days from arrival.

I asked Sapolsky whether this was of benefit to pack members. In fact, it turned out that everyone benefited from decreased aggression.[250] According to Sapolsky, the blood pressures of pack members decreased, and they had less stress hormones in their blood. In addition, less conflicts also meant less infection prone wounds, and moreover, with pack members grooming each other more often and more diligently, everyone had less parasites and more time to look for food. Sapolsky believes that this is because the females were more relaxed and less afraid, as aggressive males were not dominating the pack or venting their frustration on the females.

Sapolsky finds no support in natural selection for a style of leadership based on hierarchical aggression and competition: "Based on extensive research, we know that natural selection is not based solely on aggression or competition. There are many species among which there is little aggression, where hierarchies are not significant, and even if they exist, they are built from the ground up (i.e., if a dominant individual acts violently, it will be driven out of the pack). For males, competition is not the only strategy for successful mating. Animals have complex cooperation networks based on reciprocity. The idea that nature is red in tooth and claw has, in other words, been decisively challenged."

---

250 Comments based on correspondence with Robert Sapolsky in February 2014, as well as Sapolsky's article "A Natural History of Peace" in *Foreign Affairs*.

Therefore, nature is perhaps not as singularly violent and straightforward as many believe. Sapolsky is particularly wary of using this kind of model from nature in order to justify how human beings are to be led. "My own understanding is that there are no scientific grounds to assume that examples derived from animals concerning for example hierarchies, leadership positions and aggression would tell us anything about what is natural or inevitable for human beings."

As Sapolsky has stated, there are no scientific grounds for drawing a direct comparison between pack animals and human beings. However, it would be equally wrong to claim that we would have transcended our evolutionary history. Indeed, if you look at this from the perspective of everyday events, you can find almost unlimited examples of how human packs work. These packs are called workplaces, project teams, gangs, families and – why not – sports teams. A pack can act like Robert Sapolsky's Forest Group or like an ordinary pack of baboons.

When one draws together Sapolsky's observations, and the thoughts and findings of Stephen Porges discussed earlier, one finds a significant point of convergence: baboons and people act differently when they feel safe, and this change in behaviour seems to benefit all concerned. One can of course succeed using either method, but at a different cost. With cooperation, one's blood pressure stays at a healthy level and one only occasionally has surges of stress hormones, while with the other stress hormones are a constant. In the first, pack members are in many important respects equal and cooperative, while in the second one member dominates the group. In one, there is a constant sense of danger, while in the other – according to what is perhaps Stephen Porges' most important idea – members mainly feel safe, and open up in a new way to social interaction as the environment turns out to be a safe one.

Cooperation should not be war, and intimidation should not be a leader's main tool. Furthermore, as the examples in this book show, the opposite method does not have to be a soft, hippie utopia.

Not Another Burning Platform

1.

On 1 June 1971, President Nixon stood soberly in front of the press. He had an important message to the nation – he had found the true enemy of the US: drugs. In his speech, Nixon made it clear that drugs were public enemy number one. He declared a war on drugs.[251]

This speech was underpinned by a real problem: over 40,000 US soldiers fighting in the Vietnam War were addicted to drugs.[252] Who knows, Nixon may even have been concerned about these soldiers. Nevertheless, it is more likely that the reason for his pronouncement was much closer to home. Support for the Vietnam War had continued to plummet, critical voices had gained more ground, and anti-war protests were reaching a new peak. Nixon had promised to secure an honourable exit from the Vietnam War, but this turned out to be an empty promise. The situation was very awkward for a man hoping to get reelected. Attention had to be diverted elsewhere, and the nation had to be mobilised.

---

251 Nixon's speeches can be found in many sources, for example at: https://www.youtube.com/watch?v=jc47fMU8sf8; https://www.youtube.com/watch?v=jc47f-MU8sf8 and https://www.youtube.com/watch?v=jtZaWLOSiWA. One can also find many descriptions and analyses of the war on drugs, for example Ed Vulliamy's "Nixon's 'war on drugs' began 40 years ago, and the battle is still raging," The Guardian, 24 July 2011.

252 This subject has been studied by journalist Tom Feiling, who has written on the subject in his excellent The Candy Machine: How Cocaine Took Over the World (2009).

Nixon combined voters' fears with the notion that something had to be done about the situation. The war could be fought and won, and volunteers could participate. However, unlike Vietnam, this war would not require sacrificing one's life or the lives of one's children, but just voting for Nixon. The President asked Congress for 84 million dollars of emergency funding. He was re-elected by a landslide, and the war on drugs was on.

Now, over 40 years later, this war can be deemed a failure. Nixon's fear-laden message did not solve the real problem. There is a record number of arrests, the jails are full of drug sellers and recreational users, but the use of cocaine and other drugs has not decreased. Based on the results, the champions of the war on drugs did not find an intelligent or creative solution to the problem. Of course, this may not even have been the purpose. Perhaps the biggest motivator was to mobilise voters, and by creating an atmosphere of fear, Nixon accomplished just that.

2.

Nixon's actions illustrate the two-fold nature of fear. Fear, like any other strong emotion, creates the need to act, unless the emotion is strong enough to make people freeze up. Fear can mobilise the masses, make cancer patients change their living habits, urge company employees to change their behaviour, and bring protesters to the barricades. Fear also forces people to focus on the problem. This might be the main reason why fear is often used as a management tool and as a core method in the struggle for power.

The problem with fear is that it doesn't necessarily make people more intelligent. Usually the opposite. As acting often seems more important than what actions is taken and whether it is effective, people are often unable to pay attention to how rationally or intelligently they act under the influence of fear.

Companies also face the risk that, by using intimidation and making employees afraid, company staff – while they do concentrate on the threat and take action – lose their best cognitive capabilities and creative edge when it comes to problem solving.

For some reason, this side of the story has not reached the corporate world. It is still common to increase crisis awareness and pressure in companies where cognitive abilities have already collapsed, fear freezes communication and the best employees are soon packing their things. Managers believe that crisis awareness should be increased in order to mobilise the masses. They talk about a "burning platform," i.e., a burning oil-drilling rig, onto which they have to get their employees in order to effect change. The silliest thing about this widely disseminated notion of leadership is that it is based on a misunderstanding.

3.

The fire on the Piper Alpha oil rig, moored off the coastal waters of Scotland, was breaking news in July 1988. One hundred and 67 oil rig employees and two rescue personnel were killed in the fire, which was the worst accident in five decades of oil drilling in the North Sea. Journalists from around the world covered the disaster. One survivor, Andy Mochan, jumped from a height of fifteen stories into the sea. Meanwhile, Daryl Conner was watching the burning oil rig on the TV. He was writing a book about leadership. He had been looking for a good metaphor for some time in order to best describe a change in people's attitudes. The events leading to Andy Mochan's escape gave Conner what he had been looking for. According to Conner, Mochan told a TV reporter that he had two options at the time: either to jump into the sea or to burn alive. He chose, and jumped, even though he did not want to. Thus was born the widely (and erroneously) used management phrase "burning platform."

The term was so sexy that it quickly spread among consultants and managers. The burning platform was originally supposed to describe a leader's commitment to change, but gradually it started to mean something else. According to Conner, the two most common misunderstandings about the term are that a situation would need to be catastrophic before successful change can be effected, and that a manager should consciously manipulate information in order to create a pressing need for change.[253] Conner encountered misuse of the term so often that he decided to write a series of blog posts in order to restore the original meaning.

In other words, according to the apologias of its inventor, the burning platform does not mean that a company would only succeed at changing if it is on the brink of, or in the middle of a disaster. It also does not mean that a leader should manipulate information in order to get employees to get a move on. What it actually means is that a leader must take responsibility for the change.

---

253 Connor writes about this misunderstanding and the background of the term in his series of blogs "The Real Story of the Burning Platform" at www.connerpartners.com.

Steve Kotter is another management consultant whose ideas have been used to justify intimidation. He is one of those who have misused the burning platform. Kotter's own term "sense of urgency" is a phrase that (when misunderstood) is used to refer to how managers effect change by increasing crisis awareness. However, Kotter is also, at least these days, of the view that when a platform is set on fire, one of the possible consequences is that those on the rig die in the fire.[254]

These days, platforms are set on fire on a constant basis, but usually the ones who burn are the employees, not the management.

4.

One of the most famous users of the term "burning platform" is Stephen Elop, former CEO of Nokia. He led Nokia into a historical period of change with his famous letter on the state of the company. "I have learned that we are standing on a burning platform. And, we have more than one explosion – we have multiple points of scorching heat that are fuelling a blazing fire around us."[255] The memo was followed by Nokia moving to the Windows platform, and finally selling its devices unit to Elop's past and present employer, Microsoft.

Both the examples of Nixon and Elop seem to suggest that there are situations where intimidation works extremely well. In other words, situations where a leader wishes to get his way and where

---

254 Source: http://www.forbes.com/sites/johnkotter/2011/04/21/why-a-fear-based-culture-will-never-drive-true-change/

255 Source: http://blogs.wsj.com/tech-europe/2011/02/09/full-text-nokia-ceo-stephen-elops-burning-platform-memo/

others are not expected to engage in creative problem solving – all that is expected is compliance with the wishes of management. Nixon's true intention was not to solve the drug problem, but to get re-elected. When it came to Stephen Elop, it fitted his aims and economic interest to receive a mandate for a simple solution, i.e., transferring to the Windows platform, which in the end cost many, many jobs. Fear is an effective way to get a mandate.

Intimidation seems to work in situations where there is only one clear solution that is already known, whether that is to start a war, to change living habits, to redirect resources, to jump off a burning platform or to vote for the right candidate.

One possible reason for this has been offered by neuro-economist Gregory Berns in *The New York Times*. Berns organised an experiment for his colleagues where test participants received mild but painful electric shocks. Participants quickly learned to fear the shocks, but according to Berns the true aim of the experiment was that test subjects, fitted with imaging equipment, were made to wait for the shocks. The time between shocks was 1-30 seconds.

The parts of test subjects' brains responsible for handling pain were activated, unsurprisingly, when test subjects were subjected to shocks. What was surprising was that these same areas were also activated when subjects waited for the shocks. According to Berns, fear appeared to consume so much brain power that waiting for, handling and enduring pain took energy away from other neural processes. Berns claims that the most important practical finding of neural research on fear is that when fear-related systems are initiated, investigatory behaviour and risk taking immediately cease.

Which also means an end to creative problem solving.

5.

Unfortunately, Stephen Elop was not the first top manager to use fear as a tool at Nokia. There was a long history of fear-based leadership and management in the company.

A recent paper by Timo Vuori and Quy Huy suggests that the main reason for Nokia's decline was fear.

Vuori and Quy describe how middle managers and top management had different fears, but when those fears were combined, it sent the company on a downward spiral to a corporate culture of desperately avoiding internal risk taking. Nokia grew into intelligent dumber organization by violently shutting down or ignoring anyone who raised concerns about how realistic the schedules were and whether they had the technical capabilities required to reach set targets.

Vuori and Huy interviewed 76 top and middle managers, engineers and external experts. They concluded that top managers were afraid of external competitors. Top management was in shock after the launch of Apple's iPhone. Top management then turned on the pressure cooker for their subordinates to get new, innovative products out faster to meet market demand, which in turn led to crippling internal fear among middle management. According to the employees and experts Vuori and Huy interviewed, top management did not communicate the severity of the external threat clearly. They mainly communicated about what and less about why. After the pressure was on, top management grew increasingly frustrated when someone raised any doubts about the organization's technical capabilities, or voiced any critical notions regarding their objectives. Top management's aggressive attitude towards criticism eventually blocked them from getting the information that would have revealed the true internal state of the company. Top management was too optimistic, and middle management began to search for scapegoats for future failures.

This fear-based culture helped yes-men to get more power in the organization, and when the yes-men realized that they could not in any case meet their targets, they lurked under the radar of top management and waited until someone else had to come clean, and then shifted the blame for failure onto some poor middle manager and his team. Everyone knew that someone would fail because everyone accepted unrealistic targets. Consequently, the best strategy to save your ass in middle management was to say yes to upper management's demands, keep the reality of things to yourself and wait for someone else to crumble.

This was not the beginning of Nokia's fear-based culture in Nokia. Even before the new reality on the smartphone market hit Nokia, there was a strong base for a culture of fear. Vuori and Huy found numerous examples of widely shared stories about past aggressive behaviour by top management. Memories of these stories triggered intuitive fear reactions in middle managers, since they were on the lower rungs of a very hierarchical organization. It was smart to keep your mouth shut when the pressure was on. If Vuori's and Huy's paper is representative of the whole organization, it looks like most of the middle managers were in survival mode. – not a good place to be if you are expected to be at your most creative.

It was not only top management that had an aggressive and dismissive leadership style. According to Vuori and Huy, Jorma Ollila, the former CEO of Nokia and at the time the chairman of the board of the company, was extremely temperamental.

According to stories shared inside the company, Ollila would go around shouting at people at the top of his lungs so that the "target's balls shrank."

Everything that happened inside and outside Nokia fed the culture of fear. It spread in the organization, and soon people could sense it from small but obvious clues. People who were typically open, had trouble expressing themselves freely with certain top managers. They fell quiet and their voices shook when they spoke.

The pressure inside Nokia was insane, especially for those who felt that Nokia was their only viable ticket to status and financial security. They were the ones that had gone all in, and they were the ones who were mainly responsible for the company's more innovative products. On the other hand, they were also the ones who were frozen by the pressure and the fear of losing their standing in the organization.

Reading through Vuori'sand Huy's paper, one gets the impression that fear and excess pressure surely put people in Nokia on a (misunderstood) burning platform even before Stephen Elop's famous letter. And although it pushed people to do something, it didn't make the company more intelligent or creative –on the contrary. It made the company and the intelligent people that worked there work at the lower range of their capabilities. It made the company stupid.

One of the outcomes of the different forms of "burning platform management" is that company employees are subjected to constant stress hormones for no good purpose. Management drives employees onto burning platforms, hoping that this will result in more activities appropriate to the company's aims, as well as more problem solving and responsibility. Instead, management finds people locking up and problems getting worse. The mood becomes anxious, there is less cooperation, most people suffer a decrease in cognitive ability – as a consequence, management becomes ever more frustrated. Some employees give up, as it would be absurd to sink resources into a project that cannot succeed. Working days become exercises in endurance, and some start to wait for the bitter end. If management succeeds in encouraging movement, it may turn out to be the movement of employees out of the firm. In the worst case scenario, top talents, sick of cortisol-laced work days, leave the firm. Those employees capable of finding jobs elsewhere do so. Those left on the platform sink into an ever deepening mire of anxiety: some try to get by, others freeze completely, while yet others search for at least some kind of solution to their pain. Even getting fired or facing bankruptcy are better options than dwelling in limbo.

Despite all of the above, crises, worry or fear cannot and should not be entirely disregarded when it comes to effecting change. What is important is to split fear into portion s, and to be aware of contexts and risks. Fear of failure may lead to a person practicing or studying more diligently, and fear – in proper doses – can be a motivating force. When company employees hear that the company is to undertake a strict austerity program or to face unprecedented competition, but they are at the same time presented concrete issues that they can affect, people generally get cracking. I have personally seen this many times in the course of my work. What is essential is the experience of being able to affect a crisis. In some cases, an external threat makes a group more close knit. However, even then it seems to be important that a sufficiently large number of community members believe that the external threat can be beaten.

6.

In the hands of the wrong person, fear can be a powerful but unpredictable weapon. However, reaping the benefits is never certain, while the detriments are almost certain.[256] This kind of behaviour amounts to playing Russian roulette with the ability of individuals and communities to endure stress. Even though fear is an easy way to grasp power and to encourage the need for change and make people focus, it should be the last, rather than the first and primary tool in a leader's arsenal for, among other things, the threat it poses for the health and work capacity of the people affected.

Of course, there are also situations where intimidation serves the ends of a manager. These situations do not require creative problem solving, as there is only one, predefined solution, as in the cases of Nixon and Elop.[257]

The thought that a leader should manipulate people through fear or trigger employees' defence mechanisms in order to make them concentrate on what is essential, to launch a change or to fend off an unwanted change, should at the very least be seriously re-examined. Instead of intimidation, it would be more humane, and often more profitable for managers to first think about the question presented in the beginning of this book: how would people behave if they were not afraid?

---

256 For example, due to constantly elevated stress hormone levels.

257 Of course, I do not claim that the move to the Windows platform would have been Stephen Elop's primary or original aim. However, it is a fact that this move definitely did not harm Elop's personal career or finances.

Epilogue

1.

When Kiwi[258] movie director Cameron Duncan started filming his short movie *Strike Zone* in 2003, he knew it would be his last. It was not that the young would be director, only 17, did not want to make more movies. The fact was that he was sick with bone cancer.[259] Two months after starting filming, Duncan died.

Duncan's last short film was in a way a last will and legacy. He wrote the script for the movie in his sickbed, and directed the movie himself, ignoring the severe pain caused by the final stages of his illness. He also played the lead in the movie, starring under his own name. In the film, the protagonist sits at the doctor's office, only to hear the doctor say the words he had been dreading: the cancer had returned, and the treatments were no longer working. He had only two months to live.

This turned out to be Duncan's fate in real life as well. His cancer was discovered in 2002, and after a series of heavy treatments, he became well for a moment. However, after two months his cancer came back and this time it was lethal.

---

258 Nickname for the people of New Zeeland

259 Duncan was sick with an osteosarcoma, a very rare and aggressive form of cancer, the cause of which is unknown. Most patients with osteosarcoma are young or over 60.

In *Strike Zone*, the protagonist uses his last two months to form a softball team[260] and to coach them to victory. The film is in many ways overblown and unsubtle, but it has also drawn amazed comments from some critics at the director's astute observations on life.[261]

In the movie, Duncan reflects on his own life at the very end of it, and hopes that he did "something worthwhile" with his life. When the team needs their coach's guidance at the decisive moment, he gathers them together and addresses them one last time: "I want you to pitch the hardest your arm will let you throw the ball. I want you guys to run the fastest and the hardest that your legs will carry you, because if there's one thing that I've learned from all I've been through is that you only regret the things you didn't do. No regrets. Not tonight."[262]

The movie ends with the death of the lead character and his funeral. From the grave, the view pans to a softball field. During the scene, Duncan speaks calmly, stating that he wants to be missed and for people to cry at his funeral. Right at the end of the movie, Duncan says that he does not want to be forgotten – and that he thinks "he's done a pretty good job with that."

---

260 Cameron Duncan wanted to be a softball pro.

261 Director Peter Jackson and his wife Fran Walsh met Cameron Duncan while filming *The Lord of the Rings: The Return of the King* in New Zealand. They were both very impressed with Duncan's talents. They also provided filming gear and staff for Duncan for the infomercial he was shooting for an organ donor campaign. Duncan was buried, as seen in the film, in a place overlooking a softball field. According to some sources, the song *Into the West* (performed by Annie Lenox, melody by Howard Shore and words by Fran Walsh), which was inspired by Duncan's story, was performed at his funeral for the first time (from a recording). Walsh and Jackson also decided to share Duncan's story and his two short movies in the extra materials provided with the ex-tended edition of the DVD for *The Return of the King*. The same DVD also included a separate documentary called *Cameron Duncan – The Inspiration for Into the West.*

262 Cameron Duncan: *Strike Zone*, 2003.

Falling seriously ill at such a young age forced Duncan to think about things that many address only much later in life. Imminent death makes you think about what is important and meaningful.

2.

Duncan's insights are further supported by Bronnie Ware, an Australian nurse who has spent years working with terminally ill patients. Ware's book Top Five Regrets of the Dying list the five most common regrets of the terminally ill. The regrets of the dying have a direct connection to Duncan's views, even though most of Ware's patients had lived long lives.

According to Ware, people on their deathbeds regret not being brave enough to make their own choices. They also wish that they had worked less, that they would have had the courage to express their feelings, that they would have kept better in touch with their friends, and that they would have allowed themselves to be happy.

Fear is involved in many of the regrets featured in the book. It had an influence on Ware's patients' choices, with a heavy cost. Even though fear felt like an important and sensible guiding factor when making choices, at one's death bed it seems like an almost absurd basis for a decision – it is almost as if fear is a relevant criteria only when it feels like one has almost unlimited time. The moment that time starts to run out, fear seems to lose all meaning.

Making one's own choices, or rather not making them, was according to Ware the most common regret. This also caused the most frustration among Ware's patients, as they had realised it too late. Some also regretted having submitted to others or having let others' expectations dominate their own decisions – resulting in mediocre lives. During their lives, they were unable to find out what they would have been capable of, as they were afraid to express or fulfil their desires. Some were afraid of change, and consequently were stuck with their old habits and limitations.

Furthermore, fear stopped many of Ware's patients from saying how they felt. Many had been afraid that it would cause strife with others or make them look ridiculous. Many were also troubled by fear of revenge or humiliation. Ware's list went on. Some patients had become addicted to their own careers. The status brought by their careers was addictive, and it felt bad to give up the respect and influence it had brought. As one male, career addicted patient put it: "I wish I could have ignored what others thought about me, as I can now. I don't understand why we have to wait for death before realising something like this."

It is interesting to take a close look at the fears of Ware's patients and to assess how important or real the various fears that guided their choices were, and what remains of them when the heart strikes its last beat and the neural impulses of one's brain cease. This may be a liberating thought, as it makes us ask: why do we feel that fear-induced thoughts are important right now?

3.

The chapters of this book share two themes. The first is a question: how would we act if we were not afraid? Years ago, I put this question to my friend, who was weighing the various choices she had made in her life. Since then, she has gotten into the habit of asking herself this question, and I am happy to say that she is so far satisfied with the choices she has made. However, the more important thing is for us to stop for at least a moment, switch off the autopilot, and notice how and why fear affects what we do and fail to do. If I have been at least partly successful in writing this book, then perhaps this monster will cease interfering so much with the choices of other people in addition to my friend. Perhaps there are at least a few readers who will not have regrets during the last few weeks of their lives for not having dared to express themselves or for not living the life they wanted to live.

The second theme is a task that I took when I started writing this book. I have done my best to try and take away the mystique of fear, to turn it into an ultimately concrete phenomenon that can be tackled in many different ways. I have tried to expose the monster both where it works slyly in the background and where it has already revealed itself.

Fear memories can affect a person's mental health, social fears can isolate, and a workplace's alpha boss can destroy a worker's self-esteem for years. Therefore it appears to be crucial to understand in what circumstances fear is like a test to be passed, and where individuals and communities should shield themselves from it, to avoid its most extreme effects.

There are fears that one must learn to face in order to cope at the workplace and to stay sane. Coping with uncertainty and facing new people and social situations are everyday challenges for almost everyone involved in working life. However, there are also more destructive fears. Humiliation, cheating, mind-games, social games, destructive competition, having new ideas shot down, psychopathic leaders, intimidation for power, fear-laced organisational structures, being branded as a failure, and taking joy in other people's shame are the hallmarks of a sick, or at least problematic community.

When one takes a closer look at fear, it becomes increasingly apparent that fear is in the end something that is a very much concrete phenomenon, and furthermore that different fears are in fact variations on the same themes. It seems that the feelings and physiological changes classified as fear are caused by uncertainty and unpredictability, the threat of failure, the thought of losing something, encountering fears that one has faced before or just thinking about them, genetically programmed threats and even experiencing the sensation of fear itself.

4.

It is comforting and liberating that one can actually do something about fear. It is therefore stupid that we do not rein in fear where it clearly works against our aims. When you take away its mystique, fear becomes something concrete, something that can be handled. There are some eminently, perhaps surprisingly straightforward means to defeat or harness fear: building tolerance, exhaling more slowly, practicing under pressure, changing fear memories, rebranding experiences and lowering the stakes in a frightening situation. Furthermore, these methods do not really require years of practice or even much in the way of therapy. Most of them are basic tools; even an amateur builder can achieve something with a saw, hammer and spirit level even without extensive professional training. The same analogy applies with fear.

An individual has primary responsibility for resolving his or her own fears. Nevertheless, in order to defeat or harness fear, one needs more than just individual commitment: community action. I tend to think that half of the actions necessary to remove fear can be undertaken by the individual, but the rest is up to the community, and particularly those in positions of authority or power. However, the surrounding community, bosses and colleagues have at least an equally large role in eradicating fear.

I have learned much while writing this book, but as I stated in the beginning, it has not led to my becoming fearless or assuming complete control of my defensive system. Furthermore, it is not even something I would aspire to. I am still afraid of making mistakes, of hitting a moose on the motorway, and for the safety of my children. When standing on a rickety rope bridge, my body still goes into overdrive. However, what matters is what one does when fear strikes. Will I submit without a fight and pay the cost of fear, or will I fight the monster?

Appendices

Appendix 1: Causes of Fear

Uncertainty and unpredictability are always connected with the future. Freddie Mercury and BrewDog show what can at best happen, when one dares to step onto uncertain, unpredictable territory. However, at the same time we all know what has happened to so many who stepped onto uncertain ground. Explorer Robert F. Scott and his crew died on their expedition to the South Pole, expiring of exhaustion, hunger and exposure in 1912 (they did in fact reach the South Pole, only to find that Roald Amundsen's group had been there before them). The same fear of uncertainty and unpredictability can, however, also be caused by everyday things like a person being unwilling to go watch improvisational theatre because she cannot know in advance what might happen. One can be genuinely and deeply afraid of failure and the shame that goes with it. However, it can be equally uncomfortable to live in uncertainty due to not knowing what might happen in the future on an emotional level. What if you suddenly freeze, start throwing things around, or burst out in tears in the middle of everything?

Threat of failure may lead to shame, and having unrealistic ideas about yourself. Jukka Perko was driven to practice by threat of failure. However, he defeated this threat, because he had a solid practice routine and a little random luck due to happening to practice under pressure. However, Perko has also said that he plays better when he dares to let go of this sensation of protective fear. When he stops controlling and making sure, the skills he has accumulated during practice became fully available when he needs them. Would be entrepreneurs are also afraid of failure, and often give up on the idea of starting their own business. As shown by Caroll Dweck, threat of failure can be mitigated by adopting a growth mindset, where victories and losses lose meaning, and everything is feedback.

The thought of losing something seems to be deep-rooted in us. We look at things with the presumption that everything is permanent. We achieve a certain reputation, we have a job or a successful business, we are rich or we have found the perfect wife or husband. However, we will ultimately lose all of this in any case – it is just a question of when. If one looks on these things as assets, one must constantly live with the fear of loss.

Previously encountered dangers or vivid images thereof are recorded in our brains. As Daniela Schiller has written, fear-related associations are located in the amygdala. We human beings are special in that we can be afraid of things we have never encountered. We can also learn to be wary and fearful of things learned from other people's stories, and which may in fact be completely harmless.

Threats we are genetically programmed to recognise, some of which we might never have encountered. For example, half of mankind is afraid of snakes and spiders even though many of these people live in areas without dangerous snakes – or snakes full stop. In addition, fear of heights and perhaps even some of our social fears seem to be genetically programmed into us. According to experts, these fears stem from the distant past of our evolutionary history.

Experiencing fear itself is painful. It quite simply does not feel nice when your heart is racing, your brain slows down, your chest hurts and you start to hyperventilate. Even though fully experiencing this sensation often also extinguishes it, it is a painful way to get rid of fear.

Appendix 2: Methods for an Individual to Control and Defeat Fear

Building tolerance is quite simply the most effective way to treat fear. However, one must be willing to accept that building tolerance may feel uncomfortable for a long time. For example, it took three years for Urpo Koponen with the adders. It may take hundreds of practice sessions in order to get rid of stage fright. However, one must take comfort in the fact that the sensation of fear will eventually change. As Markku Niemivirta has noted, we are not doomed to live eternally with this feeling. If a person builds tolerance in frightening situations, fear will in the end be conquered.

Using the vagal brake is more or less the only effective way to take control of an already initiated fear reaction. It also helps in situations where building tolerance is undertaken in real-life, stressful circumstances. One can slow down one's exhalations in order to take control of nervous reactions in many different situations. For example, even people prone to violence in difficult situations are taught to calm down by using the vagal brake by the simple expedient of counting to three when breathing in, and to six when breathing out.

Practicing under pressure can be used to teach the brain how to operate under pressure. Increasing the stakes in practice situations or using mental images seem to work much the same way as building tolerance, with the exception that in this case building tolerance is not done in real situations, which means that the emotional cost of failure is not high.

Changing fear memories is one of the most interesting findings presented in this book. Based on Daniela Schiller's research, fear memories can be altered. In other words, even if the received wisdom is true and one cannot change history, one can at least change how one feels about that history today.

Rebranding an experience also seems to be against common sense, but in practice and as proved in research, it is an extremely effective method. You can switch from one highly strung emotion to another by rebranding the emotion. Even though this may seem impossible or improbable, you can change the negative effect of fear by interpreting the high activation state of your body as excitement.

Lowering the stakes is, as a psychological method, one of the most effective and workable. I personally experienced it while behind the wheel of an F1, by comparing the danger I was in with the motor biking I do every summer. However, one can lower the stakes in many other ways as well: by using a fly on the wall or historical perspective, by reducing the importance of a situation, by focusing on the moment or even by changing the situation into a learning experience. Stephen Porges' findings concerning the nature of play may also be applied to lower the stakes. When we feel that we are in some way in control of a situation, the danger and related fear present in that situation seem in some strange way pleasant. This interpretation is often within our own grasp.

Appendix 3: Methods for a Community to Control and Defeat Fear

Complete openness and transparency make leading through fear impossible, as the best gravitate to workplaces where the work atmosphere is humane – which in turn affects who gets selected for management. There may still be space for psychopaths, but less of it than otherwise.

Creating a safe space is more or less everybody's responsibility. Emotions are contagious, and we can consciously stir certain emotions in others. After having acquired this power, one can also decide what kind of emotional states one wishes to push on other people. Conductor Benjamin Zander asked others to ask him: who am I, if the eyes of the people around me are not shining like they were deer in the headlights?

Fostering trust is often best done by taking shared risks. Management can also affect what kind of story it tells within the company.

A story where failures are feedback leading to learning may help a community to preserve its belief in the future, which is vital.

Removing the stakes helped the Crystal Palace Eagles to rise from their mire in the 1st Division to the Championship. It is a good method particularly when crisis awareness is already wide spread, and is clearly starting to paralyse the community.

Focusing only on what you can do is a method that good leaders have employed during the present economic downturn. If the organisation is not producing results, then focusing on that only weakens self-esteem and increases fear of the future. Small things that one can concretely do strengthen the belief that one can really affect things. Concreteness is poison for fear.

More dialogue, less debate increases group intelligence. Teams and groups can for example make an agreement about how to interact, and to discuss those thoughts and feelings that arise in social situations. Group intelligence can be increased by cutting down on vicious comparisons and by distributing speaking turns more equally.

Appendix 4: The Economic Effects of Fear Relating to Entrepreneurship

Harri Hietala, 31 July 2014

Below, I have calculated the economic effects of obstacles to launching a company, in particular fear of failure. I have also presented the dynamics of this phenomenon, and drawn some inferences on long-term effects on employment and GDP (ceteris paribus).

One out of four persons of working age, i.e., aged 15-64, is interested in entrepreneurship. Of these, less than one in five actively considers starting a company. Finally, about one in ten of this last group actually does start a firm. However, some of these firms never start business operations, but rather remain inactive. (Pajarinen & Rouvinen: *Mistä yrittäjät tulevat?* 2006; ENG: *Where do Entrepreneurs Come From?*). Tekes Teknologiakatsaus 198/2006).

Of launched firms, many stop operations within the first few years due to lack of profitability; two in three companies stop within the first 10 years, half already during the first five years. (*Statistics Finland: Yritysrekisterin vuositilasto sekä aloittaneet ja lopettaneet yritykset; ENG: Annual statistic for the register of companies as well as launched and lapsed firms.*)

According to Amway, of all adults, fear of failure accounts for approximately 70% of those who are obstructed from becoming entrepreneurs (Amway: Global Entrepreneurship Report, 2013). However, let us assume that a smaller proportion applies to those who have gone forward to actually consider founding a company: 35%. The actual percentage varies from survey to survey depending, e.g., on the questions asked. However, this percentage is in any case conservative as a measure of the amount of people who do not become entrepreneurs due to fear of failure.

Based on current annual net growth in Finland (approximately 4,000 entrepreneurs/firms) we have reached a base of 260,000 entrepreneurs/companies (Statistics Finland, Työvoimatutkimus (ENG: Labour study) [number of entrepreneurs]/Yritysrekisterin

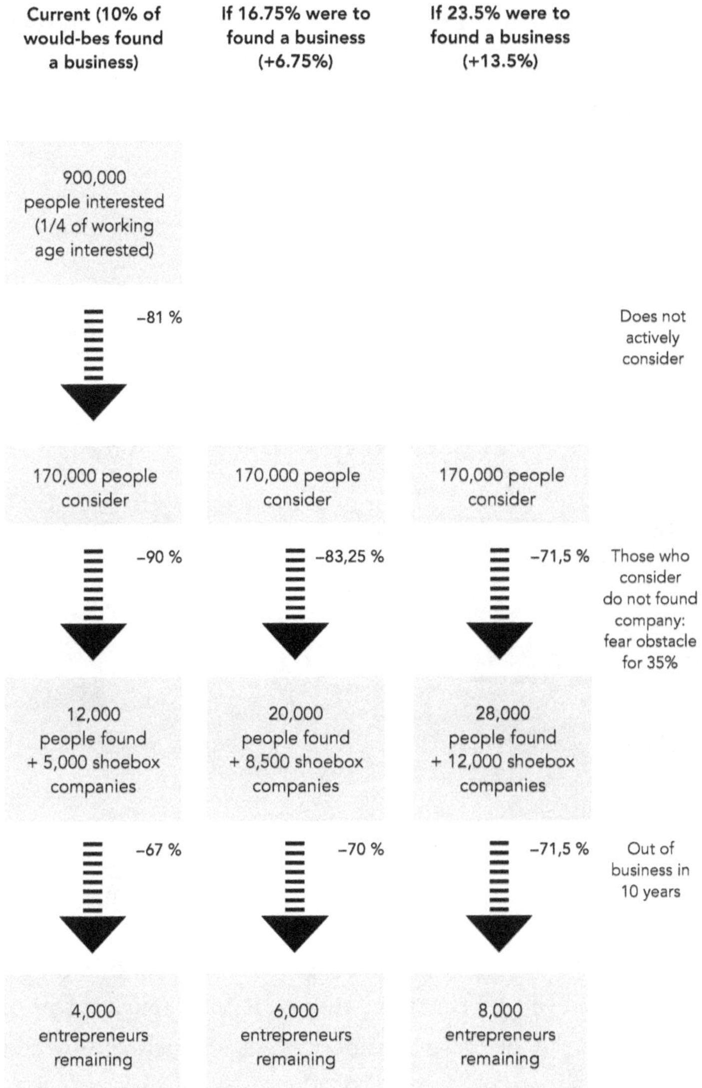

vuositilasto (ENG: Annual statistic for the register of companies [number of companies]). The amount of people working was

2,480,000 (employment rate 69%) in such a way that 2,146,000 of this number were employees and 91,000 were employer-entrepreneurs (169,000 one man companies) (Statistics Finland, Työvoimatutkimus (ENG: Labour study).

	Currently 10% start	If 16.75% started	If 23.5% started
Working age	3 600 000	3 600 000	3 600 000
Working	2 480 000 (69%)	2 725 000 (76%)	2 970 000 (82%)
Salaried	2 146 000	2 261 000	2 376 000
Entrepreneurs	260 000	390 000	520 000
Sole entrepreneurs	169 000	254 000	338 000
Employers	91 000	136 000	182 000
GDP	193 mrd. €	212 mrd. €	231 mrd. €
GDP per capita	35 600 €	39 000 €	44 000 €

Now if one were to assume that (from the beginning) net growth had been 1.5 times larger, with for example less fear of failure (16.75,% of those considering entrepreneurship would have become entrepreneurs), this base would have grown to 390,000 entrepreneurs/firms (+130,000) and the amount of people working would be 2,725,000 (+245,000, +10%) (employment rate 76%). There would be 2,261,000 employees (+115,000) and 136,000 employers (+45,000) (254,000 one man companies).

If one were to assume that (from the beginning) net growth would have been 2 times larger, with for example less fear of failure (23.5% of those considering entrepreneurship would have become entrepreneurs), we would now have to 520,000 entrepreneurs/firms (+260,000) and the amount of people working would be 2,970,000 (+490,000, +20%) (employment rate 82%). There would be 2,376,000 employees (+230,000) and 182,000 employers (+91,000) (338,000 one-man companies).

The amount of people working has been estimated with the assumption that the proportion of employees (35%) would remain constant, but the size of small and mid-sized firms acting as employers would be smaller than before: 1.7-2 employees, rather than the present average, 2.5 employees.

If productivity were to remain the same over these different scenarios (smaller units might mean slightly less productivity, though on the other hand increased competition and disruptive enterprises [creative destruction] changing old production methods could increase productivity), GDP would be ten or twenty percent higher. Therefore, our present GDP of EUR 193 billion would be EUR 212 or 231 billion in the two scenarios above, which would mean per capita GDP of EUR 39,100 or 44,000, instead of EUR 35,600. (Statistics Finland, *Kansantalouden tilinpito*; ENG: *Accounts of the national economy*).

In other words, the "value" of one entrepreneur for increasing the Finnish GDP is almost EUR 150,000 per year. An increase of one per cent to the number of entrepreneurs (260,000) would in other words mean an almost EUR 400 million (0.2%) increase in GDP.

If obstacles to starting a business were to be reduced according to their current proportion, i.e. if 35% of starting entrepreneurs were to launch a business due to no longer being afraid of failure, a one per cent increase of starting entrepreneurs from those who consider starting a business would amount to an EUR one billion increase in annual GDP in the long term, due to decrease of fear of failure as an obstacle.

Appendix 5: Point of Interest of a Company

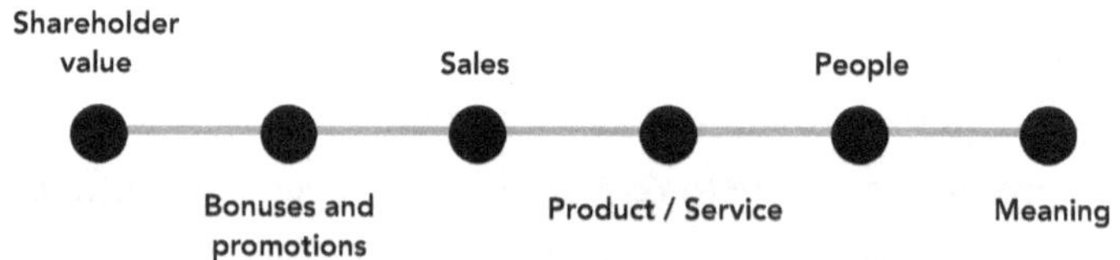

Appendix 6: Typical Features of Archetypes

	Archetype I (Heroic leader)	Archetype II (Mature leader)
Worldview	Deism	Zen
Perspective/worldview	Black and white	Pluralistic
Attitude to people's failings	Impatient	Patient
Basis for decision making	One truth	Curiosity
Driving force	Fear	Meaning
Method for involving others	Manipulation	Dialogue
Motive	Thirst for power	Desire to get things done
Mood	Guilt	Trust
Decision making	One decision maker	At all levels
Energy	Patriarchal	Matriarchall
Selection	According to tolerance	According to merit
Model of development	Creation story	Evolution
Amygdala	Activated	Not activated
Prefrontal cortex	Locked	At full capacity
Model for success	Star players	Team
State of nervous system	Fight / flight / freeze	Social interaction

Acknowledgements

The impulse for writing this book came from the people I met while working with various companies. I discovered that fear is the obstacle that stops companies, teams and individuals from reaching their full potential. Therefore I thank all of these people who dared to speak about difficult things, to face up to their own shortcoming and to try something new and dangerous even when every cell of their bodies was screaming no.

I would like to thank my dear wife Jenni for her support, frank comments and help with translations. I would also like to thank my three daughters for their support and for being who they area. I would like to thank all four of you for the love you have shown me.

I owe an immense debt of gratitude to those people who have contributed their time and energy to reading and commenting on the various versions of this book. A big thank you to Marjaana Toiminen for the irreplaceable and vital help she gave me particularly with the first versions of this book. Thank you, Hanna Jensen, for your attention to detail and for your incisive comments. Thank you, Yrjö Mähönen, for help with the medical material, Johanna Ijäs for the psychological material, and Markku Niemivirta for scientific commentary and for sparring with me over the materials. However, I wish to emphasise that there are flaws in this book, which are mine. Thank you, Fredrik Rahka, for your support and warm criticism, as well as Saku Tuominen, Elias Koskimies, Tuomas Enbuske and Anna Dahlman for your astute observations and ideas. I also wish to thank my editor,

Ilona Räihä, for her views, patience and professionalism. Thank you, Janne Metso, for help with the background for this book.

A big thank you to all interviewees: Dr Stephen Porges, Dr Daniela Schiller, James Watt of BrewDog, biologist David Sapolsky, saxophonist Jukka Perko, the unfortunate "Leila," Hanno Nevalinna of Futurice, researcher Uri Nili, Jenn Lim of Deliver Happiness, snake photographer Urpo Koponen, serial entrepreneur Taneli Tikka and Aki Riihilahti, the Eagle of Crystal Palace. A special thanks to economist Harri Hietala for his calculations.

I am grateful and amazed for all the support and friendship I have been shown.

www.ingramcontent.com/pod-product-compliance
Lightning Source LLC
Chambersburg PA
CBHW051248250726
48656CB00004B/1186